"*Short of Glory* is an exceptional introduction [...] esis 3 are woven through the biblical witness [...] acumen and exegetical sophistication are front and center as he carefully elucidates the far-reaching implications of sin and the even farther-reaching implications of God's grace to his people. Highly recommended as an example of theology and exegesis in service of the good news."

Brandon D. Smith, Assistant Professor of Theology and New Testament, Cedarville University; Cofounder, Center for Baptist Renewal

"We often speak of living in a 'fallen world.' But what does that mean, precisely? In order to embrace the good news of the gospel, we first have to understand the problems that Jesus came to fix. In this penetrating reflection on Genesis 3, Mitchell Chase helps us see every aspect of life as, to quote Tolkien, 'soaked with the sense of exile.' *Short of Glory* will help us better appreciate how comprehensive the work of Christ is—and make us long for it to be completed."

Gavin Ortlund, Pastor, First Baptist Church of Ojai, California; author, *Finding the Right Hills to Die On* and *Why God Makes Sense in a World That Doesn't*

"Understanding what went wrong is essential for understanding how it can be made right, and by whom. Mitchell Chase expertly guides readers not only through Genesis 3 but also through the reverberations of Genesis 3 in the rest of the Scriptures. The tentacles of the fall can be felt on every page of the Bible. Not paying attention to these themes might mean missing what the good news is all about."

Patrick Schreiner, Associate Professor of New Testament and Biblical Theology, Midwestern Baptist Theological Seminary; author, *The Visual Word* and *The Kingdom of God and the Glory of the Cross*

"We live in a world of turmoil, heartache, and evil. We know it shouldn't be so, but we don't always spend enough time reflecting on why it is. As this book helps us to stare at the greatest of all tragedies, two things start happening: we see the world in much sharper clarity, and we find ourselves drawn again and again to the hope of Christ."

Sam Allberry, pastor; author, *7 Myths about Singleness*

"Mitchell Chase's book is refreshing because he retrieves the covenant of works to explain why original sin must be traced back to Adam as our federal head. Plunging into the sorrow of Adam's iniquity, Chase then lifts our heads to see the hope we have in Christ, our covenant surety. Unless we understand the tragedy of our fall in Adam, we will not rejoice at the triumph of our redemption in Christ, the second Adam. Here is a compelling exposition of our exile east of Eden."

Matthew Barrett, Associate Professor of Christian Theology, Midwestern Baptist Theological Seminary; Executive Editor, *Credo Magazine*; author, *Simply Trinity*

Short of Glory

Also from Crossway by Mitchell L. Chase

Resurrection Hope and the Death of Death

Short of Glory

A Biblical and Theological Exploration of the Fall

Mitchell L. Chase

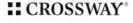

CROSSWAY®

WHEATON, ILLINOIS

Trade paperback ISBN: 978-1-4335-8509-8
ePub ISBN: 978-1-4335-8512-8
PDF ISBN: 978-1-4335-8510-4
Mobipocket ISBN: 978-1-4335-8511-1

Library of Congress Cataloging-in-Publication Data

Names: Chase, Mitchell L., 1983– author.
Title: Short of glory : a biblical and theological exploration of the Fall / Mitchell L. Chase.
Description: Wheaton, Illinois : Crossway, 2023. | Includes bibliographical references and index.
Identifiers: LCCN 2022037957 (print) | LCCN 2022037958 (ebook) | ISBN 9781433585098 (trade paperback) | ISBN 9781433585104 (pdf) | ISBN 9781433585111 (mobi) | ISBN 9781433585128 (epub)
Subjects: LCSH: Bible. Genesis, III—Commentaries. | Fall of man.
Classification: LCC BS1235.5 .C49 2023 (print) | LCC BS1235.5 (ebook) | DDC 222/.1106—dc23/eng/20221115
LC record available at https://lccn.loc.gov/2022037957
LC ebook record available at https://lccn.loc.gov/2022037958

Crossway is a publishing ministry of Good News Publishers.

BP			32	31	30	29	28	27	26	25	24	23
15	14	13	12	11	10	9	8	7	6	5	4	3	2	1

For Mike Senior,
my friend and colaborer
in the ministry of good news

Contents

Acknowledgments

THE TASK OF WRITING REQUIRES THINKING, and we find out how clearly we think about things when we write about them. I have been edified through the process of thinking about the glory that God has made us for, as well as the fall in Genesis 3, which had a profound effect on the remainder of Scripture's storyline and on all of our lives.

Every writing project connects to names of those who were vital before, during, or after the writing process. I'm grateful for Samuel James's encouragement about this book from the very start. His guidance and input were valuable, and I'm honored that he and the good folks at Crossway have trusted me with this project.

During the writing process, my wife, Stacie, provided helpful comments on every chapter. I'm inspired by her patience and insight. She is a daily gift in a hundred different ways. I'm thankful that Cody Floate read a draft of the manuscript as well, setting aside time to give thoughtful feedback.

I have dedicated this book to Mike Senior, who is my fellow elder and friend. I first met Mike in 2012 when I became the preaching pastor at Kosmosdale Baptist Church in Louisville, Kentucky. He sets an example in the way he loves and cares for his family and his church. What a blessing to labor in ministry alongside such a brother, whose heart seeks the kingdom! We often smile together about a remark from R. C. Sproul in reply to an anonymously submitted question from the audience many years ago during a panel discussion. Sproul's response has shown up on coffee mugs and social media ever since: "What's wrong with you people?" Well, Mike, this book answers that question.

Introduction

WHEN A FLOATING SHELF FELL from our living room wall, we heard multiple sounds at the same time. The small clay pot cracked, the frame with the picture crashed, the shelf itself was especially loud, the candleholder clattered, and a short rectangular wooden sign whacked the floor. Sitting in the living room as this happened, my wife and I jumped up to intervene and deal with the mess. It turns out that one of our sons had been on the other side of the wall and banged it at the right—or wrong—spot, causing the shelf to shift and collapse under the weight of its contents.

Not every fall is the same. But the more items involved and the greater their weight, the louder the crash and more numerous the sounds.

What would a breaking world sound like? And how long would the sounds of such a fall last?

The Scene That Changed Everything

Genesis 3 gives Bible readers the explanation of what happened between Genesis 2 and 4. The middle chapter ushers us into different conditions. In Genesis 2, the man and woman are together and without shame and in covenant with each other. The garden has plentiful

1

food, there is a commission to multiply and subdue, and there is a benevolent Creator, whose words of wisdom will be life and peace for his image bearers. Then in Genesis 4, an older brother murders his younger brother, and this tragedy happens after the elder's sacrifice is rejected while the younger's is accepted.

What explains the transition from peace to tragedy? What accounts for the rise of wickedness? The content of Genesis 3. It's the scene that changes everything for everyone. It's the part of the movie that has such explanatory power, you're just confused if you return after leaving the room for a few minutes.

During a series of talks addressing temptation, D. A. Carson once said:

> What's the importance of Genesis 3 to our thinking? The primary importance is that it sets the stage for the entire Bible storyline. Problems and solutions must match. If you want to understand what the Gospel is about, what Jesus is about, what the cross achieves, then you must understand the nature of the problem they address.[1]

There are different ways to conceive of the Bible's storyline. You can think of the Old Testament as what anticipates Jesus and the New Testament as what announces his arrival. You can view Scripture as the epic of God's redemptive story where he promises, advances, and then fulfills his plan to raise up a Savior for sinners. You can notice how the Bible begins with the story of creation and ends with the hope of new creation.

---

1 D. A. Carson, "The Temptation of Adam and Eve" (lecture given as part of a series entitled "The Christian Life: Fighting Temptation," Bethesda Baptist Church, Allen Park, Michigan, August 27, 2013).

One helpful and popular way to conceive of the Bible's storyline is with four words: *creation, fall, redemption, consummation*. What would consummation mean without our understanding of what was reaching a culmination? We need the category of redemption in order to make sense of the biblical story. And yet we know that redemption isn't something needed because of creation. The story of creation was about our good God making a good world. He didn't make a broken world.

When we look around us and within us, a truth is clear: not all is well in God's world and in God's image bearers. We see destruction, disease, and death. We see wickedness and false worship. Signs of corruption—ethically and physically—are everywhere. Things are not the way they once were or will be. In the order of creation, fall, redemption, and consummation, the unpleasant reality of the fall is evident. We must grasp it, process it, reflect on it.

The word *fall* is shorthand for the rebellion and repercussions that began in the garden of Eden in Genesis 3. The fall is what happened to God's creation, and it's why there is a need for redemption. We live as fallen people in a fallen world. The hope of consummation tells us that the conditions of the fall are temporary. All things will be made new, even though that's not the way things look right now.

To grow in our understanding of the Bible's big story, we must think about the fall. We must know what happened, why it happened, and what followed.

Ground for Later Growth

Maybe you already think you know what happened in Genesis 3. "Adam and Eve rebelled against God in the face of temptation," you say, "and then judgments followed that have affected us all ever since."

But would you be willing to think more deeply and slowly about this chapter, connecting its themes with the rest of Scripture?

All of us are born outside Eden, so Genesis 1–3 is a special set of chapters. God makes the world, and specifically a garden, for his people. And there, in the sacred space of Eden, God's image bearers defy his word and succumb to the tempter. When God exiles them, we are exiled in them too. Yet, in that same chapter where God announces judgment, he gives a promise of hope that a deliverer will come one day and defeat the serpent.

The rest of the biblical story grows out of the ground of Genesis 3. When we meditate on the content of this chapter, many biblical themes and connections become clear. The events in Genesis 3 become a lens through which to read and understand the progressive revelation of God's redemptive epic.[2]

Think of Genesis 3 as containing seeds of various kinds. There are temptation and shame and coverings. There are a tree of wisdom and one of life. There are messianic hope, the reality of death in the dust, and exile from sacred space. There are blame shifting, hiding, and a response of faith. If we will spend time thinking about the intricacies of Genesis 3 and the interconnections across Scripture, we will see how pivotal this chapter is in the biblical storyline, and we will recognize the many notions that grow out of the garden ground.

If we situate the fall in Scripture's storyline effectively, an exploration of Genesis 3 will result in greater joy in the good news about Jesus. By tuning our ears to creation's groanings, our hope will be stirred along the way. In Romans 8, the apostle Paul says:

2 According to T. Desmond Alexander, "The events of Genesis 3 are exceptionally important for understanding the biblical meta-story." *From Eden to the New Jerusalem: An Introduction to Biblical Theology* (Grand Rapids, MI: Kregel, 2008), 102.

Creation waits with eager longing for the revealing of the sons of God. For the creation was subjected to futility, not willingly, but because of him who subjected it, in hope that the creation itself will be set free from its bondage to corruption and obtain the freedom of the glory of the children of God. (8:19–21)

While Genesis 3 announces the subjection of creation to futility, that status is not permanent. Corruption will give way to new creation by the power of God. If you are in Christ, did you know that your future is glory?

As we study Genesis 3 and its innerbiblical connections and consequences, my prayer is that your hope will be stirred, that you will join the groans of creation longing for liberation. Genesis 3 records tragedy, yes, but it doesn't record only that. Interwoven amid deception and fig leaves and exile is a hope for a future Son. Tragedy is mixed with hope, and one day that hope became flesh and dwelt among us.

1

Sacred Space

WHEN I THINK ABOUT A GARDEN, I have memories from child-
hood. My maternal grandparents had a garden every year, and I helped
till rows, plant seed, and pick produce. And in my earliest conception
of the garden of Eden, I pictured rows of dirt and an assortment of
growing plants. What I didn't imagine was sacred space like a sanctuary, yet that would have been more accurate.

An Expandable Sanctuary

One way to tell the story of the Bible is with the theme of sacred space.
It's the kind of theme that locks the metanarrative together. Sacred
space is given, lost, promised, and at last received again. As readers
cross the threshold into Genesis 3, they come to a sacred place that God
gave his people. God had made the heavens and the earth (1:1–25), and
part of his work on earth included a garden in a place called Eden (2:8).

We shouldn't conceive of Eden as a walled and bounded space. At
the same time, though, Eden comprised only a small place in the ancient Near East. Conditions in Eden were not like conditions outside
Eden. Part of the judgment in Genesis 3 was exile from the garden

(3:22–24). Furthermore, in the middle of the garden were the tree of life and the tree of the knowledge of good and evil (2:9), and these trees wouldn't be accessible once exile happened.

According to the creation commission in Genesis 1:28, God told his image bearers, "Be fruitful and multiply and fill the earth and subdue it, and have dominion over the fish of the sea and over the birds of the heavens and over every living thing that moves on the earth." Multiplication and dominion were key to this commission. What would happen as Adam and Eve had children and those children had children? Expanding generations would mean filling up the sacred space of Eden.

It is reasonable that expanding generations implied an expandable sanctuary as well, especially if part of the commission was to subdue and exercise dominion. Subdue what? Exercise dominion over what? Since the conditions outside Eden wouldn't have matched life inside Eden, the task of Genesis 1:28 was to bring the glories of Eden to the rest of the earth. When Revelation 21–22 depicts a transformed heaven and earth radiating with the glory of God, we are seeing a vision of Eden's goal, the trajectory set in the garden paradise.

The sacredness of Eden is confirmed by the tasks God specified: "The Lord God took the man and put him in the garden of Eden to work it and keep it" (Gen. 2:15). Not just to "work" and not just to "keep"—both tasks were the plan. These terms occur in the Old Testament independently, but when they appear together, we can notice a context of priesthood. To "work" means to "serve" or "minister," and to "keep" means to "guard." For example, the Lord said:

> Bring the tribe of Levi near, and set them before Aaron the priest, that they may minister to him. They shall *keep guard* over him and over the whole congregation before the tent of meeting, as they

minister at the tabernacle. They shall *guard* all the furnishings of the tent of meeting, and *keep guard* over the people of Israel as they *minister* at the tabernacle. (Num. 3:6–8)

And from the age of fifty years they shall withdraw from the duty of the service and *serve* no more. They minister to their brothers in the tent of meeting by *keeping guard*, but they shall *do no service*. Thus shall you do to the Levites in assigning their duties. (Num. 8:25–26)

And you shall *keep guard* over the sanctuary and over the altar, that there may never again be wrath on the people of Israel. And behold, I have taken your brothers the Levites from among the people of Israel. They are a gift to you, given to the LORD, *to do the service* of the tent of meeting. (Num. 18:5–6)

Reading the Pentateuch as a whole, we can see that the priestly instructions had precedent in Adam's garden responsibilities. More than a farmer attending to rows of crops, Adam was a priest in sacred space, charged with serving and guarding, or working and keeping, Eden.[1] As J. V. Fesko put it, "Adam's mandate is not merely to labor but to expand the garden-temple throughout the earth, fill the earth with the image of God, and subdue it by spreading the glory of God to the ends of the earth."[2] Knowing this about Adam, we can see his priestly failure in Genesis 3.

---

1 Meredith Kline says, "God produced in Eden a microcosm version of his cosmic sanctuary. . . . It was the temple-garden of God, the place chosen by the Glory-Spirit who hovered over creation from the beginning to be the focal site of his throne-presence among men." *Images of the Spirit* (Eugene, OR: Wipf and Stock, 1998), 35.

2 J. V. Fesko, *Last Things First: Unlocking Genesis 1–3 with the Christ of Eschatology* (Fearn, Ross-shire, Scotland: Mentor, 2007), 102.

The scene in Genesis 3 involves the entrance of a deceiving crea-ture into Eden. The dialogue and events of that chapter resulted from Adam's failure to serve and guard the garden sanctuary effectively.

Adam was to "subdue" and "have dominion over the fish of the sea and over the birds of the heavens and over every living thing that moves on the earth" (Gen. 1:28). The serpent in Genesis 3 was a creeping thing "that moves on the earth," and Adam should have exercised dominion over it.

Genesis 3 records, among other things, the defilement of sacred space.

A Promise of Land

God exiled Adam and Eve from Eden, and he placed cherubim on the eastern entrance to guard it (Gen. 3:24). Adam had failed to guard the sanctuary ground, so God appointed cherubim who wouldn't fail at the job.

Mankind multiplied outside Eden, and there is no account of any-one entering it after Genesis 3. Bible readers have often wondered what happened to that garden land near four ancient Near Eastern rivers. No biblical author tells of its destruction, but the flood in Genesis 6–8 probably destroyed it. We shouldn't imagine that currently somewhere in the ancient Near East is a place called Eden with cherubim guard-ing its eastern entrance.

In one sense the biblical storyline leaves Eden behind, but in a truer sense it doesn't. The notion of sacred space continues, and the reverberations of Eden echo in later Scripture. God's design was that his people dwell with him in a place set apart for his glory. This hope is echoed in God's promises to Abraham in Genesis 12. God said to him, "Go from your country and your kindred and your father's house to the land that I will show you" (12:1). Abraham's nephew Lot traveled with him and "saw that the Jordan Valley was well watered everywhere like the garden of the LORD" (13:10).

Just as God relocated Adam to a place (the garden of Eden), he would relocate Abraham to a place (the promised land). And this place would be filled with a fruitful family. God said, "And I will make of you a great nation" (Gen. 12:2). Abraham would be a new Adam with the task of multiplying in and filling up a specific place. In order to understand the importance of the promised land, we must see it in the context of the first couple's separation from Eden.

In Genesis 12, Abraham arrives at this land and travels through it, building altars and worshiping the Lord. The promised land plays a crucial part in the Bible's storyline because it is an instance of sacred space where God's word and glory are to be obeyed and treasured. Though Eden was in the past, the hope of Eden continues.[3] God will have a people as well as a place for them.

The Holy Space of the Tabernacle

Long after the exile from the garden of Eden, and approximately six hundred years after Abraham received precious promises about a people and a place, God rescued the Israelites out of Egypt and brought them to Mount Sinai. There at the bottom of the mountain, they constructed what God had directed them to build: a portable tent of meeting, called the tabernacle, where God would manifest his

---

3 When the book of Isaiah provided comforting words to distressed Israelites, part of God's comfort was that God would make the promised land like Eden. "For the LORD comforts Zion; / he comforts all her waste places / and makes her wilderness like Eden, / her desert like the garden of the LORD; / joy and gladness will be found in her, / thanksgiving and the voice of song" (51:3).

holy presence and glory in the midst of the people he had redeemed (Ex. 35–40).

A large courtyard surrounded this dwelling place, and the entrance was on the eastern side. When the priests entered the tabernacle itself, they entered the large room known as the Holy Place, and its entrance was also on the eastern side. Progressing deeper into the Holy Place, only the high priest could go into the last room—the Most Holy Place (or Holy of Holies). He would enter it once a year on the Day of Atonement (Lev. 16).

Israelites could enter the courtyard, only priests could enter the Holy Place, and only the high priest could go behind the veil into the Most Holy Place. These levels of access reflected increasing holiness, as people approached the God who tabernacled among sinners. Degrees of access were reminiscent of Genesis 1–2. God had created the earth, and on earth was a place called Eden, and in Eden the Lord planted a garden. The existence of the tabernacle was about holy space. This space was holy because God is holy. Those who entered the tabernacle had to be set apart as his holy priests, and they were to represent the nation of Israel, which was called to be a holy people.

For those who lamented the loss of Eden, the tabernacle was a glimpse of glorious news: our holy God could draw near to sinners. Though cherubim prevented Adam and Eve from returning to Eden through the eastern entrance, the tabernacle had an eastern entrance to picture image bearers coming back into the presence of God. This portable tent was a visible reminder of the hope of Eden.

In fact, as the Levitical priests entered the tabernacle, they did so under curtain coverings that had artfully designed cherubim woven into them (Ex. 26:1). And the veil that separated the Most Holy Place from the Holy Place was also designed with cherubim on it (26:31).

As the high priest went behind the veil on the Day of Atonement, no cherubim with flaming swords blocked his way. Rather, the Lord—who is a consuming fire—received him, and in receiving him the Lord was receiving those whom he represented.

The high priest acted as a new Adam, crossing through the cherubim and entering the presence of a holy God.[4] Like Adam, the priests were to serve and guard the tabernacle. The place was a sanctuary and holy; thus it was sacred and echoed Eden.

Cleansing and Dwelling in Sacred Space

The book of Joshua narrates the keeping of God's promises made earlier to Abraham. The Israelites—Abraham's descendants—were inheriting the land of promise. Their responsibility was to serve as a kingdom of priests in a land that needed to know the Lord. God warned against becoming like the nations and taking on their gods. Instead, the Israelites were to maintain true worship and covenant faithfulness, setting the example of what it meant to be image bearers of the Creator.

The challenge of inheriting the promised land was that it was occupied with idolaters. Some of these idolatrous peoples would seek Israel's destruction, so God announced ahead of time that he would give the land to his people. They did not need to fear the inhabitants of the land. The Israelites only needed to trust the Lord and persevere as they beheld his steadfast love and faithfulness.

---

4 As Michael Morales puts it, "The later high priest of Israel serving in the tabernacle must be understood fundamentally as an Adam-figure serving on the (architectural) mountain of God." *Who Shall Ascend the Mountain of the Lord? A Biblical Theology of the Book of Leviticus*, New Studies in Biblical Theology 37 (Downers Grove, IL: InterVarsity Press, 2015), 53.

Subduing the Canaanite combatants, as well as demolishing the idolatrous shrines and pillars and altars, was part of cleansing sacred space. The uncleanness of immorality and false worship had pervaded the land, and the Israelites were to exercise dominion so that the glory of the one true God would be esteemed and loved.

The conquest in the book of Joshua focuses on Canaan, for that was the land God promised to Abraham. And yet the goal of the conquest was much larger. As Israel occupied Canaan and subdued idolatry, they were eventually to expand. The expansion of sacred space recalled the goal of the garden: the worldwide worship of Yahweh. By teaching and upholding and modeling true worship, the Israelites would be serving and guarding sacred space, a place where the knowledge of God was to spread so that the nations might honor him in their repentance and belief.

When the Israelites crossed the Jordan into Canaan, the tabernacle crossed with them. This tent of meeting was portable for a reason, that the Israelites could carry it to the land of promise. Once in Canaan, the portability of the tabernacle was no longer essential. Something more stable could be built. King Solomon oversaw the construction of the Jerusalem temple (1 Kings 5–8). And this temple replicated the degrees of access that led into the Most Holy Place, where, behind the veil, only the high priest could go.

While the tabernacle was replaced by the temple, the latter—like the former—echoed Eden.[5] Through eastern entrances, the Israelites were led into the presence of God through his appointed representa-

---

5 According to T. Desmond Alexander, "Linked to both Eden and the cosmos, the tabernacle, as a model, conveys the idea that the whole earth is to become God's dwelling place." *From Eden to the New Jerusalem: An Introduction to Biblical Theology* (Grand Rapids, MI: Kregel Academic, 2008), 41–42.

tives (the priests). The presence of the temple meant that Jerusalem was the most important city on earth. Moving outward, we can think of this holy city and then the land to which it belongs and finally the earth on which the land exists.

The ability to mark gradations of importance/holiness is a major reason we hear echoes of Eden. When the Israelites prepared to conquer the land in the book of Joshua, they entered it from the east, crossing the Jordan River and coming up to Jericho. The glimpses of Eden remind readers that God's redemptive plan moves forward, and that human sin will not prove to be an insurmountable barrier to him. Whenever a priest went into the courtyard or the Holy Place or even behind the veil, the picture was being redrawn of image bearers ascending into the presence of the God who made them and loves them and has come for them.

Seated with Christ as Heirs of the World

The first coming of Christ brought inauguration, and his second coming will bring consummation. Part of his inaugurated work is the spiritual rest and citizenship that are true for all his people. We have "come to Mount Zion and to the city of the living God, the heavenly Jerusalem" (Heb. 12:22). These spiritual realities are profoundly true and yet are only the beginning.

What has begun is important, nevertheless. According to Hebrews 1:3, the ascended Christ "sat down at the right hand of the Majesty on high," and according to Ephesians 2:6, we have been "seated" with Christ "in the heavenly places." Already we have rest in Christ (Matt. 11:28–30). But ours is a rest that isn't yet finished. Our union with Christ has not exhausted the fulfillment of God's people dwelling in sacred space for his glory. Union with Christ has brought the inauguration of certain things, and it also guarantees their consummation.

Abraham and the patriarchs all died in faith, "not having received the things promised, but having seen them and greeted them from afar, and having acknowledged that they were strangers and exiles on the earth" (Heb. 11:13). Believers who die have this in common with Abraham: they die in faith, not receiving the fullness of God's promises.

Knowing the promises that Abraham and his offspring would inherit a land, Paul used global language to identify the fulfillment: "For the promise to Abraham and his offspring that he would be heir of the world did not come through the law but through the righteousness of faith" (Rom. 4:13). Heir of the *world*? Let me immediately affirm that Paul hadn't misunderstood the Abrahamic covenant. He rightly understood what God's promises to Abraham ultimately entailed. Like Eden, the land of Canaan had a trajectory: that the knowledge and worship of the living God would cover the earth as the waters cover the seas (Hab. 2:14).

God had spoken to Abraham about a certain land, but the heirs of God's promises would receive far more than that property. That sacred land foreshadowed the global renewal of all things. Remember Jesus's beatitude for the meek? He said, "Blessed are the meek, for they shall inherit the earth" (Matt. 5:5). The *earth*. Not just the land of Canaan. Not just space that was marked by certain regions and bodies of water. Jesus's promise for the meek is that they are heirs with Abraham of the world.

God's plan is not about returning his image bearers to the paradise of Eden. He will do more and better than that. The believer's hope for the future is the joining of heaven and earth. This coming marriage is the goal of Eden, and it is the climax of the Bible's storyline. In Revelation 21–22, all things become new. The forever home of God's people is a transformed and glorified cosmos. The current intermediate state of deceased saints will give way to a final and everlasting state of immortal embodied life in a place that God has purified by his power.

The longing for this better country is not just a New Testament hope. According to Hebrews 11:16, the patriarchs desired a "better country, that is, a heavenly one. Therefore God is not ashamed to be called their God, for he has prepared for them a city." The storyline of Scripture takes us from the garden to this glorified city. In one of John's visions, he "saw the holy city, new Jerusalem, coming down out of heaven from God, prepared as a bride adorned for her husband" (Rev. 21:2).

When God makes all things new, "No longer will there be anything accursed, but the throne of God and of the Lamb will be in it, and his servants will worship him" (Rev. 22:3). The new heaven and new earth are depicted as a glorified city. And unlike the old Jerusalem, where a temple stood, in the new Jerusalem there will be no temple, "for its temple is the Lord God the Almighty and the Lamb" (21:22).

Sacred space will be the pervading reality. There will be no gradations or levels of access. The new Jerusalem is a city behind the veil. The events in Genesis 3 did not derail the redemptive plan of God to lead his people to the city that is to come. There will be no exile from that blessed new creation land because our union with Christ brings everlasting citizenship. The dominion of Christ with his people will be total, and it will never be undermined by the serpent. Of that place we're told that "nothing unclean will ever enter it" (Rev. 21:27).

This Christian Life

The geographical context of Genesis 3 is the garden of Eden, but the context for our lives is different. We live in a post–Genesis 3 world.

Like the end of the Bible's storyline, our future is the new Jerusalem. We are already citizens there, so we are pilgrims going home. Can't you sense and see disarray in the world? Doesn't the glorious hope of new creation ignite your heart? The presence of Eden's sanctuary should direct our desires.

What is lost in Genesis 3 will be redeemed. God will once again dwell with his people in a sacred place, and things like the tabernacle, the temple, and the land of Canaan foreshadowed this hope. When we notice the theme of sacred space in Scripture, we can rest assured that God will not forsake us. Meditate on the glories of Eden, for they point to greater glories still to come.

"Under the sun"—a recurring phrase in Ecclesiastes—we face trials of various kinds. Our passing years involve one loss after another—health, jobs, finances, friends, family. We need to know that these earthly troubles do not have the last word. By thinking about the Bible's storyline that takes readers from the garden to the lasting city, we can understand where to plot our own lives. We can be hopeful in a fallen world, for God has made his people heirs together with his beloved Son. Along with Abraham and all the redeemed, we will inherit the earth.

Two Trees

WHERE DO YOU KEEP THINGS that are important to you? Location can communicate value. Think of why people use safes or lockboxes. There might be items you'd display in your kitchen or living room but never leave out in your front yard. The location we choose for certain things can signal their importance.

God planted a garden, and out of the ground trees sprung up that were pleasant to the eye and good for food. The biblical author emphasizes the location for what comes next: "The tree of life was in the midst of the garden, and the tree of the knowledge of good and evil" (Gen. 2:9).

Paying Attention to Trees

I used to think that one of these trees was good and the other bad. But after God created the world and filled it with animals and the first two image bearers, he pronounced it good—indeed, "very good" (Gen. 1:31). There were many trees that were good for food and pleasant to look at (2:9), but something was different about the two trees in the midst of the garden. The biblical author gives them extra attention.

Looking carefully at these two trees, we can make at least seven observations. First, these were good trees made by a good God. Second, the different names of these two trees imply that they were not the same kind of tree and that they both were different from the other trees that had sprung up from the ground. Third, both trees are mentioned in Genesis 2 and 3. So, in order to understand what happens in the latter chapter, we need to know the setup in the former chapter. Fourth, there is a command associated with the tree of the knowledge of good and evil (Gen. 2:17). Fifth, these two trees bore fruit that could be eaten and, when eaten, would produce different outcomes. Sixth, after Adam and Eve ate from the forbidden tree, they were denied access to the other one. Seventh, the relevance of these two trees extends beyond Genesis 3.

Of all the trees in the garden of Eden, God gave a prohibition concerning one of them. He told Adam, "You may surely eat of every tree of the garden, but of the tree of the knowledge of good and evil you shall not eat, for in the day that you eat of it you shall surely die" (Gen. 2:16–17). The prohibition was followed by an explanation, a warning about death. Because the Lord had not made Eve and yet she would allude to this command in conversation with the serpent (3:3), Adam must have communicated God's words about this forbidden tree.

Since what the Lord made was good, the forbidden tree was not forbidden for being bad. Instead, God's image bearers needed to learn to trust the Lord and to submit to his word. His commands and warnings are good for creatures who can make real choices that have real consequences.

In the garden of Eden, Adam received a command from the Lord for his good. I don't think we should imagine some kind of fruit with magical properties but rather a tree that represented submission to the wisdom of God. The forbidden tree was called the tree of the "knowledge of good and evil," and this phrase instantly connects us to notions of wisdom in later Scripture, such as the book of Proverbs. The wise know the difference between good and evil, and they pursue what is good. Wisdom is more than intellectual discernment. The wise apply what they know in skillful living for God's glory.

The tree of the knowledge of good and evil represented divine wisdom. The presence of that tree was a reminder that God's wisdom was paramount, should be trusted, and should shape the lives of his image bearers. But the presence of fruit on the tree made defiance possible. If God's image bearers took the fruit for themselves, this taking symbolized rejecting. By ignoring God's command and seizing the fruit of that tree, his image bearers would be seeking wisdom on their own terms and rejecting his authority. They would be acting independently of God's command. They would be treating God's warning ("in the day that you eat of it you shall surely die"—Gen. 2:17) as something he wouldn't really carry out or as something whose consequence shouldn't really be feared.

By taking the fruit from the tree of wisdom contrary to God's command, his image bearers would, in that act, demonstrate foolishness instead of wisdom. Eating from the tree of the knowledge of good and evil wasn't something essential to their growth in wisdom, at least not initially. Honoring God's word was essential to growing wise. And by trusting God's wisdom and honoring his commands, his image bearers would be able to make right judgments as they assessed and subdued what might defile God's sacred space.

The serpent tempted Eve with the idea of knowing what God allegedly didn't want her to know (Gen. 3:4). Franz Delitzsch speaks insightfully about this tree:

The tree of knowledge was to lead man to the knowledge of good and evil; and, according to the divine intention, this was to be attained through his not eating of its fruit. . . . But as he failed to keep this divinely appointed way, and ate the forbidden fruit in opposition to the command of God, the power imparted by God to the fruit was manifested in a different way. He learned the difference between good and evil from his own guilty experience, and by receiving the evil into his own soul, fell a victim to the threatened death. Thus through his own fault the tree, which should have helped him to attain true freedom, brought nothing but the sham liberty of sin, and with it death, and that without any demoniacal power of destruction being conjured into the tree itself, or any fatal poison being hidden in its fruit.[1]

They Became Fools

One thing that characterizes the fallen world is foolishness. Daily examples on the news and social media show that folly has infected God's image bearers. Acts of sin bring ruin and grief. People do what is right in their own eyes, taking again and again from the forbidden tree. Heavenly wisdom is rejected for the sake of worldly passions. This problem isn't just in the West or in the East. No matter which direction on a compass you travel, you'll recognize that Adam and Eve didn't leave foolishness in Eden.

One of the effects of sin is the rejection of God's wisdom and righteousness. It involves knowing the truth and suppressing it, preferring falsehood and the deeds of darkness. "Claiming to be wise, they became fools," Paul said (Rom. 1:22). That indictment was true then and

1 C. F. Keil and F. Delitzsch, *The Pentateuch*, vol. 1 of *Biblical Commentary on the Old Testament*, trans. James Martin (Edinburgh: T&T Clark, 1885), 86.

is true now. How early was it true? Genesis 3 is pretty early. Thinking they would become wise, Adam and Eve became fools.

Where else can the rejection of God's wisdom lead but to folly? If seizing the fruit represented the grasping for moral autonomy apart from God, then we have all followed in the footsteps of our first parents. We have faced the seduction of ignoring God's good commands and going our own way.

The fruit from the tree of the knowledge of good and evil was still being seized as the biblical storyline advanced. In Genesis 4, Cain killed Abel. In Genesis 6, unrighteousness and immorality occupied the hearts and actions of mankind. In Genesis 11, people settled in a plain in the land of Shinar and built a tower to reach the heavens and to make a name for themselves. These episodes, and many more, show God's image bearers grasping for the fruit of the forbidden tree. Rather than treasuring God's ways and wisdom, people embraced the ways of folly and rebellion.

In the days after Joshua and the conquest, the Israelite tribes filled their allotted places, yet they turned from the commands of God and followed the worship of the surrounding nations. The spiritual evaluation appears in the last statement of the book of Judges: "In those days there was no king in Israel. Everyone did what was right in his own eyes" (21:25). We could take the events of Genesis 3 as a lens for the era of judges and say the people defied the Lord's words and took from the forbidden tree so that they might do what seemed most desirable.

Solomon and Something Greater

Wisdom is found and cultivated by submitting to the good and righteous commands of God. In 1 Kings, Solomon is presented as a new Adam who will enjoy his dominion and honor the Lord in the sacred space of the promised land. For our purposes, Solomon's request to the Lord reminds us of the failure of Genesis 3.

God said to the son of David, "Ask what I shall give you" (1 Kings 3:5). Solomon replied, "Give your servant therefore an understanding mind to govern your people, that I may discern between good and evil, for who is able to govern this your great people?" (1 Kings 3:9). The Lord answered Solomon's request, giving him a wise and discerning mind: "And God gave Solomon wisdom and understanding beyond measure, and breadth of mind like the sand on the seashore, so that Solomon's wisdom surpassed the wisdom of all the people of the east and all the wisdom of Egypt" (1 Kings 4:29–30). His wisdom became part of his reputation: "And people of all nations came to hear the wisdom of Solomon, and from all the kings of the earth, who had heard of his wisdom" (1 Kings 4:34).

Against the background of Genesis 3, Solomon's story is especially interesting, but here at last is an Adam-figure who conducts himself with wisdom. He knows good and evil, but his discerning mind is a gift from the Lord. He didn't get wisdom by turning from the Lord's command and going his own way. Wisdom was a gift from the Lord, that Solomon might know good and evil.

A reader familiar with the accounts of Solomon's life knows where his path is going. Solomon does eventually turn from the good commands of Yahweh. It's as if Solomon takes the fruit from the forbidden tree, no longer willing to hold back his hand. You cannot turn from God's commands and at the same time fear his name.

God's image bearers should seek wisdom, and this search begins with the fear of the Lord (Prov. 1:7; 9:10). To fear the Lord means to reverence and honor him, to live out a love for God in all of life. When Adam and Eve ate fruit from the forbidden tree, they weren't honoring or fearing the Lord. They showed disdain for his command and a dismissal of his warning. But if we rightly understand the value of God's words, shouldn't our response show it? As God's people seek wisdom, they should do so with diligence and resolve, like seeking silver or hidden treasures (Prov. 2:4). We should call out—pray or request, like Solomon—for insight and understanding (Prov. 2:3). The promise to wisdom seekers is that

> the LORD gives wisdom;
>> from his mouth come knowledge and understanding. (2:6; see
>> also James 1:5–8)

Solomon's example and the instructions to believers in Proverbs are sufficient to show that wisdom is not found through the pursuit of moral autonomy. Rejecting God's good commands is folly, and the path of folly isn't safe or sound. You shall surely die. Wisdom involves not repeating the sin of Adam and Eve over and over. Ultimately the Lord Jesus is the embodiment of divine wisdom. Seeking wisdom will mean following Christ. In him are hidden "all the treasures of wisdom and knowledge" (Col. 2:3).

Knowing how Scripture describes Solomon's surpassing wisdom in 1 Kings 3, we can marvel at Jesus's claim about himself in Matthew 12:42: "The queen of the South will rise up at the judgment with this generation and condemn it, for she came from the ends of the earth to hear the wisdom of Solomon, and behold, something greater than Solomon is here." Greater than Solomon, Jesus is the last Adam, who is the fountain of wisdom. Knowing good and evil, Jesus never took forbidden fruit. He walked in perfect submission to the good commands of God. He's a true and better Adam and a true and better Solomon.

The Tree for Living Forever

In the midst of the garden, there was a second tree. It was called the tree "of life" because of the effect of eating its fruit. When God exiled the couple from Eden, he placed the cherubim at the eastern entrance "to guard the way to the tree of life" (Gen. 3:24). If eating from the tree of the knowledge of good and evil meant "you shall surely die," then eating from the tree of life would mean "you shall surely live." This forever life is what God referred to when he exiled Adam, "lest he reach out his hand and take also of the tree of life and eat, and live forever" (3:22).

The tree of life held out the potential of immortal bodily life. There is no report that Adam and Eve ever ate from the tree of life, though some scholars have suggested that such eating would have been permissible and had perhaps even occurred.[2] God's prohibition about eating concerned the tree of the knowledge of good and evil (Gen. 2:17). The couple was not forbidden to eat from the tree of life.

If Adam and Eve had eaten from the tree of life on prior occasions, then their exile cut them off from this vital source of life and nourishment. Access to this tree meant life; exile from it meant death. As to whether the couple ate from the tree of life before Genesis 3, we're left with speculation. Either way, exile from it meant that an escalation toward immortal bodily life would not happen.

While God's image bearers lost access to the tree of life, the hope of what that tree represented was preserved in the tabernacle. Among the aspects of Eden reflected in the design of the tabernacle, a golden lampstand stood in the largest room (known as the Holy Place). God

2   G. K. Beale, *A New Testament Biblical Theology: The Unfolding of the Old Testament in the New* (Grand Rapids, MI: Baker Academic, 2011), 38–39.

had told the Israelites to construct a lampstand with a base, stem, branches, and flowers, all out of gold (Ex. 25:31–40). The seven lamps on the seven branches would light up the Holy Place and remind Israel that God was their light.

The lampstand in the Holy Place resembled a tree. It had a trunk and branches, and it may have been a visible reminder of the tree of life that God had placed in the midst of Eden's garden.[3] Entering the tabernacle was an ascension into the presence of God, and the priests represented the nation of Israel as they stood in the light of the golden tree.

Adam and Eve had been exiled from the garden (Gen. 3:24), yet a hope for fruit from the tree of life was not voided. The tabernacle—and, in particular, the lampstand—confirmed the plan of Israel's Redeemer to bring image bearers into the light of his presence for feasting and fellowship forever.

The Tree for Wisdom and Healing

While the tree of life may be symbolized in the tabernacle, the actual wording "tree of life" occurs outside Genesis in only one other Old Testament book—Proverbs. Speaking about wisdom, Solomon says,

> She is a tree of life to those who lay hold of her;
>> those who hold her fast are called blessed. (Prov. 3:18)

This news about wisdom is a delightful surprise when we remember that God had barred access to the tree of life. God's image bearers

---

3 L. Michael Morales, *Who Shall Ascend the Mountain of the Lord? A Biblical Theology of the Book of Leviticus*, New Studies in Biblical Theology 37 (Downers Grove, IL: InterVarsity Press, 2015), 102.

need wisdom, and getting wisdom is compared to laying hold of the tree of life.

The wisdom of God is the way back to Eden. And growing in wisdom has a fruitful effect on our lives. A few proverbs teach this truth:

The fruit of the righteous is a tree of life,
and whoever captures souls is wise. (Prov. 11:30)

Hope deferred makes the heart sick,
but a desire fulfilled is a tree of life. (Prov. 13:12)

A gentle tongue is a tree of life,
but perverseness in it breaks the spirit. (Prov. 15:4)

Seeking wisdom is the path of life, and the internalization of wisdom produces life. The words and actions of those who know God are like fruit that others can receive by God's hand. And as believers walk in wisdom, they find themselves on the narrow way that leads to life. Jesus taught: "Enter by the narrow gate. For the gate is wide and the way is easy that leads to destruction, and those who enter by it are many. For the gate is narrow and the way is hard that leads to life, and those who find it are few" (Matt. 7:13–14). To follow Jesus is to experience the inauguration of the tree of life's fruit. In Christ we have been made alive, we are on the path of life, and our future is life—indeed, resurrection life, the immortal physical life that the tree of life represented in the garden.

The life-giving nourishment of the tree of life is an image picked up in Ezekiel and then echoed in the book of Revelation. The prophet Ezekiel learns of a future temple reality that transcends anything the

Israelites experienced with the physical dwellings of the tabernacle and temple. Ezekiel is learning about a new temple in a new Jerusalem. The Lord shows him that water will flow from the future temple toward the east (47:1).

> And on the banks, on both sides of the river, there will grow all kinds of trees for food. Their leaves will not wither, nor their fruit fail, but they will bear fresh fruit every month, because the water for them flows from the sanctuary. Their fruit will be for food, and their leaves for healing. (47:12)

The fresh fruit in Ezekiel 47 means renewal, a continual life that never fails. In the book of Revelation, the apostle John is shown the river of life flowing from God's throne (Rev. 22:1). And he sees "on either side of the river, the tree of life with its twelve kinds of fruit, yielding its fruit each month. The leaves of the tree were for the healing of the nations" (22:2). The language in Revelation 22:2 is an allusion to Ezekiel 47:12. The future new creation fulfills the temple imagery in Ezekiel 40–48.

The tree of life is mentioned at the beginning of the Bible and at the end. The story between Genesis 3 and Revelation 22 is how God will bring everlasting life to his image bearers, who have turned from him and gone their own way on the path of destruction. As T. D. Alexander puts it:

> No one will grow frail by becoming old in the New Jerusalem. Citizens of the new earth will experience and enjoy both wholeness of body and longevity of life. They will have a quality of life unrestricted by disability or disease. To live in the New Jerusalem is to experience

life in all its fullness and vitality. It is to live as one has never lived before. It is to be in the prime of life, for the whole of one's life.[4]

The presence of this tree in Revelation 22 is a reminder of the undeserved grace of God, who rescues sinners, sustains them with life, and makes for them a renewed place where they will dwell forever with him.

This Christian Life

The two trees in Genesis 3 should be understood in light of what comes before and what unfolds afterward. God made mankind in his image that we might thrive in sacred space with hearts delighting in his word with reverence and honor. We were made to worship. And in God's kindness, he warned about the ruin that would come if his wise words were rejected. Part of being wise will involve our discerning between good and evil, yet true wisdom is not found on the path of moral autonomy.

God created his people to walk in wisdom. Growth in wisdom will occur as we trust God's revealed words and submit our lives to them. God's people are those who taste and see that the words of God are good and that God himself is good. Surely divine wisdom is the remedy for folly in this fallen world. Yet, as long as folly seems desirable, sinners will exchange the truth of God for a lie. Paul's command is sobering: "Look carefully then how you walk, not as unwise but as wise" (Eph. 5:15).

God made us for both wisdom and life. These notions go together. Though alienated from Eden, God's image bearers still have the hope

4 T. Desmond Alexander, *From Eden to the New Jerusalem: An Introduction to Biblical Theology* (Grand Rapids, MI: Kregel Academic, 2008), 156.

of what the tree of life represented because of divine goodness and mercy that pursues them. Christ is the fountain of all life and wisdom. Life and wisdom are ours forever because Christ is ours forever. We were made for everlasting physical life in the unmediated presence of God, and that will be our future in Christ. Because of our union with Christ, this future has begun.

3

The God Who Walks

THE DANGER OF TALKING ABOUT GOD is that we have to use language that doesn't measure up. We offer adjectives and metaphors, all while trying to describe the invisible and to lay hold of the transcendent. In the Scripture, God has given us words that help. We can speak God's words to him and about him.

God has created us with imaginations, so pictures matter. He is all-seeing, yet without eyes. He is mighty, yet without arms. In the paradise of Eden, God walks.

Dwelling with God

In the ancient Near East, a temple was the house of the deity. Since the first readers of Genesis were Israelites in the ancient Near East, they would notice the depiction of God's presence in the garden sanctuary. If we keep in mind that the garden of Eden was sacred space—a sanctuary—then we would expect it to be a place where God dwells.

After Adam and Eve had eaten the forbidden fruit, "they heard the sound of the LORD God walking in the garden in the cool of the day, and the man and his wife hid themselves from the presence of the Lord God among the trees of the garden" (Gen. 3:8). The phrases about "God walking in the garden" and "the presence of the Lord God" should be understood together. The latter clarifies the former. God was present with his image bearers.

The claim in Genesis 3:8 is the only time in the Bible's early chapters where we read about God "walking." The language is metaphorical, but metaphors are meaningful. God is present with his people in a way that denotes communion and intimate fellowship. Of course, the occasion in 3:8 is unique because God's image bearers have just violated his good and righteous command. But we should understand God's presence in the garden as something Adam and Eve had earlier enjoyed. Now, given the decision they made, God's presence is not alluring to them. They flee and hide.

Though God "walks" in the garden, we should still affirm his grandeur and omnipresence. This "walking" metaphor of God's immanence doesn't undermine his transcendence. Solomon himself recognized what a temple is and isn't: "But will God indeed dwell on the earth? Behold, heaven and the highest heaven cannot contain you; how much less this house that I have built?" (1 Kings 8:27).

A temple is where God can manifest his presence, yet a temple doesn't enclose him. It's not like a lamp for a genie. The garden was a mini-sanctuary, and the uncontainable Creator could draw near to those he had made. This truth about Eden points to something true for more than just Adam and Eve. God has made us so that we might dwell with him. Fellowship with the triune God is why we exist. It's why there's something rather than nothing. It's why there was a temple, and before that a tabernacle, and before that a garden.

Short of Glory—for Now

If we have been created to dwell with God, what effect did the fall have on this? Think of sin as introducing a spiritual breach. There is a separation from God because of sin. This separation is not spatial, because there is nowhere God is not present. This separation is relational. Due to sin, God's image bearers do not naturally enjoy peace and communion with God. Due to sin, God's image bearers reject his righteous rule and wise commands. Due to sin, God's image bearers live out rebellion and impurity.

God is holy, and we are unholy. As the unholy, we cannot dwell in the presence of God. Our natures are corrupted through and through. The Scripture calls us to love the Lord with all our hearts (Deut. 6:5), yet out of the heart proceeds all manner of unrighteousness (Matt. 15:18–20). Because God is righteous and holy, the unrighteous and unholy belong outside the realm of sacred space.

The exile from Eden makes a theological point. A major consequence of sin is separation from the blessing and life of God. As people made in the image of God, we were to live for God's glory and reflect God's glory. But we have sinned and fall short of the glory of God (Rom. 3:23). As Constantine Campbell explains:

> The glory of God is the highest purpose of humanity and of creation in general. It is the greatest motivation for serving Christ, and it is the highest hope to which believers aspire. Glory is ascribed to God's person as well as his deeds—especially those involving creation, resurrection, and re-creation.[1]

---

1 Constantine R. Campbell, *Paul and the Hope of Glory: An Exegetical and Theological Study* (Grand Rapids, MI: Zondervan Academic, 2020), 254.

Yet because of sin, we do not experience or share in the glory of God.

If we had a sense of the greatness and splendor of God's glory, we would recognize that there is no greater or more desirable privilege than to share in it. What earthly riches or fleeting pleasures could compare? What social renown or power could ever come close? As Dane Ortlund says:

> We lack glory, and we know it. At every turn in everyday life we see evidence of the truth that we know, deep within, that we have lost our true glory, our real selves. We feel keenly our sense of alienation from who we were destined to be. . . . In Adam all sinned, and the tragic result is that the divine glory with which humanity was vested in Eden—the imago dei—went into meltdown.[2]

The glory of God informs the Christian's hope. Paul wrote to the Romans: "Therefore, since we have been justified by faith, we have peace with God through our Lord Jesus Christ. Through him we have also obtained access by faith into this grace in which we stand, and we rejoice in hope of the glory of God" (5:1–2).

Campbell is right:

> Since this glory of God is the object of hope, Paul may mean that believers will share in the glory of God in the eschaton. God is already glorious, to be sure, but in the future his glory will be unveiled for all to acknowledge. . . . Having been declared righteous, having peace with God, and having the standing of grace

---

2 Dane C. Ortlund, "What Does It Mean to Fall Short of the Glory of God? Romans 3:23 in Biblical-Theological Perspective," *Westminster Theological Journal* 80, no. 1 (2018): 139.

leads Paul to boast in the future hope of sharing in the glory of God at the eschaton.[3]

The unfathomable future of dwelling with God was foreshadowed by the garden of Eden where God walked with his image bearers. The relationship was not hindered by sin and not mediated by barriers or degrees of access. Adam and Eve walked with God, and God walked with them. But by sharing in sin, we cannot share in the glory of God—not on our own.

Glory Passing By

Moses wanted what people couldn't experience. He said to the Lord, "Please show me your glory" (Ex. 33:18). Being an appointed mediator for the Israelites, Moses would hear from God, and then the people would hear God's words through him. One day, before making his grand request, Moses said to God at Mount Sinai: "If your presence will not go with me, do not bring us up from here. For how shall it be known that I have found favor in your sight, I and your people? Is it not in your going with us, so that we are distinct, I and your people, from every other people on the face of the earth?" (33:15–16).

God's dwelling among the Israelites was proof, according to Moses, that they belonged to God. The divine presence meant blessing and favor and preserving power at work. Moses understood that if God's presence was not among the people of Israel, how would they be distinct from every other people on earth? The Israelites needed God among them, and this would be for the sake of the nations who needed to know the living God.

---

3 Campbell, *Paul and the Hope of Glory*, 255. The "eschaton" refers to the end and climax of God's redemptive purposes, the consummation of all things.

Moses learned that God indeed would go with them (Ex. 33:17). So he said to the Lord, "Please show me your glory" (33:18). But God told him, "You cannot see my face, for man shall not see me and live" (33:20). In their fallen state, sinners cannot savor the glory of God. To encounter such stunning majesty would kill them. This threat of death doesn't imply anything negative about God's glory, but it does imply something negative about fallen humanity. Sinful humans lack the capacity to exult in God's glory. To bring the unholy into the un- mediated presence of God would bring destruction, for the darkness cannot abide the eternal light of God.

God granted Moses's request in a different way. He told Moses to stand in a cleft of the rock "while my glory passes by" (Ex. 33:22). Moses ascended Mount Sinai, and then,

> The LORD descended in the cloud and stood with him there, and proclaimed the name of the LORD. The LORD passed before him and proclaimed, "The LORD, the LORD, a God merciful and gracious, slow to anger, and abounding in steadfast love and faithfulness, keeping steadfast love for thousands, forgiving iniquity and transgression and sin, but who will by no means clear the guilty, visiting the in- iquity of the fathers on the children and the children's children, to the third and the fourth generation." And Moses quickly bowed his head toward the earth and worshiped. (34:5–8)[4]

A revelation of God's character is, in a true sense, a revelation of glory. God has told us who he is and what he is like. And as we

4   See James M. Hamilton Jr., *God's Glory in Salvation through Judgment: A Biblical Theology* (Wheaton, IL: Crossway, 2010). Hamilton shows the profound impact that Ex. 34:6–7 has on the canon of Scripture.

respond with trust to God's revelation of his glory, we are, in a true sense, beginning to share in it already. This was true for Moses and any believing Israelite. For those with eyes to see, God was walking—though veiled—among them.

God with Them

The desire of God to dwell among his people was clear when he instructed the Israelites to build a portable house. After they completed the tabernacle, "the cloud covered the tent of meeting, and the glory of the LORD filled the tabernacle" (Ex. 40:34). The cloud would lift from the tabernacle whenever it was time to set out, and by cloud and fire the Lord guided his people throughout their journeys (40:36–38). As the Israelites traveled, they could say, "Our God is a God who walks with us." His presence was with them; his glory was among them.

Before leaving Mount Sinai, the Israelites learned the many commands and rituals explained in the book of Leviticus. Near the end of the book, the Lord promised blessings for obedience to his law and warned of punishment if the people rejected his law. Part of these words of blessing included this:

> I will make my dwelling among you, and my soul shall not abhor you. And I will walk among you and will be your God, and you shall be my people. I am the LORD your God, who brought you out of the land of Egypt, that you should not be their slaves. And I have broken the bars of your yoke and made you walk erect. (26:11–13)

This promise to "walk among you" was an echo of Genesis 3:8. God redeemed the Israelites so that he might bring them to himself. Redemption is for reconciliation. God dwelled among them in the tabernacle, and he walked with them as they journeyed. He laid claim upon them. Fellowship with God was freedom from slavery.

Under Joshua the Israelites would enter Canaan, and there in the promised land they would be God's people, and he their God. While God "walked among them" once again, the geographical context wasn't Eden. The world was still fallen, yet the truth that God had come to dwell with them was a breath of fresh hope that the loss of Eden wouldn't last forever. Though they had sinned and fallen short of God's glory, God and God alone would mend the breach.

The temple in Jerusalem solidified what the tabernacle had left portable. The dwelling place of God would now be located where worshipers would stream. The inauguration of temple worship echoed the inauguration of the tabernacle. The narrator describes what happened: "And when the priests came out of the Holy Place, a cloud filled the house of the LORD, so that the priests could not stand to minister because of the cloud, for the glory of the LORD filled the house of the LORD" (1 Kings 8:10–11).

Recalling the first couple's expulsion from Eden, readers should be astounded that a holy God has pursued sinful people. A God who walks among us is mercy indeed. Only as a response to God's grace, then, can we be a people who walk before him in communion. In Solomon's prayer dedicating the temple, he said God's servants are those "who walk before you with all their heart" (1 Kings 8:23). God's people are those who walk with God, like Enoch and Noah did (Gen. 5:24; 6:9). Walking with God means living for God's honor by trusting his promises and word. Walking with God means being shaped by the light of his wisdom and goodness.

The Old Testament gives glimpses of the good news that our holy Creator has pursued undeserving sinners with his mercy. But the Old

Testament also contains prophecies that something greater than the tabernacle and temple was coming.

God Coming for Them

The biblical prophets mainly spoke about near-horizon events to their audience. The Israelites in the promised land needed reminders about God's law and the importance of repentance. If they lived in defiance of God's law, they would face the curse of judgment and exile. The prophets, then, were God's embodied warnings, mouthpieces declaring that mercy was in store for the penitent.

God's prophets also spoke of far-horizon events, events so far beyond their own days that different empires would rise and fall before fulfillment came. Part of these prophecies about the future involved the incredible promise of God's arrival. The language would stir the hope of the exiled and oppressed people, for their earlier kings and religious leaders had been marked by unrighteousness and foolishness. The nation had been led by bad shepherds. A heavenly shepherd would do what no mere earthly shepherd could.

The prophet Isaiah tells everyone to get ready: prepare the way for the Lord. Mountains need to get low, valleys need to rise up, and crooked paths need to straighten out (40:3–4). What should everyone, including nature, prepare for?

> And the glory of the Lord shall be revealed,
>> and all flesh shall see it together,
>>> for the mouth of the Lord has spoken. (40:5)

Isaiah says glory is coming and that people shall behold it.

Whose glory? Only one answer is correct.

> Behold, the Lord God comes with might,
>> and his arm rules for him;
> behold, his reward is with him,
>> and his recompense before him.
> He will tend his flock like a shepherd;
>> he will gather the lambs in his arms;
> he will carry them in his bosom,
>> and gently lead those that are with young. (Isa. 40:10–11)

With glory and power, with tenderness and blessing, God will come.

The prophet Ezekiel makes the same promise. The resounding good news is that God will arrive with the heart and actions of a loving shepherd:

> Behold, I, I myself will search for my sheep and will seek them out. . . .
> And I, the Lord, will be their God, and my servant David shall be prince among them. I am the Lord; I have spoken. (34:11, 24)

The prophecy is that God will come to dwell with us and reign over us. The loss of Eden is not forever. The God who walked in Eden will be the God who seeks and finds and restores.

But what would it look like for God to come to us and walk among us? The way it would happen would confound the world.

God with Us

The coming of Jesus was the arrival of God. The writer John makes a claim bursting with Old Testament significance: "And the Word became flesh and dwelt among us, and we have seen his glory, glory as of the only Son from the Father, full of grace and truth" (John 1:14). The God of the garden has come to dwell with us in Christ. Glory has taken on flesh. Jesus is "the radiance of the glory of God and the exact imprint of his nature, and he upholds the universe by the word of his power" (Heb. 1:3).

The incarnation of Jesus was, as Matthew put it, "God with us" (Matt. 1:23). His birth was signaled by shining glory around shepherds (Luke 2:9). The prophets foretold that the true and greater shepherd would one day come, so how fitting that an angel proclaimed this birth to a group of shepherds. God had sent salvation through the humble birth of his only Son. He had come to bring us near and lead us home.

Something greater than the temple was here. The advent of Jesus, through a humble and bloody birth, was greater than the smoke and thunder of Sinai and greater than the cloud and fire that led Israel out of Egypt. The hands of God healed the lame and the diseased. The words of God rebuked the demons and the stormy winds. The compassion of God welcomed the outcast and the neglected. The feet of God walked all around the promised land to bring good news.

The walking God displayed glory not only on land. In Mark 6, the disciples of Jesus were on a boat without him. Late into the night, Jesus began walking on the sea toward them. The narrator says, "He meant to pass by them" (6:48), but this didn't mean Jesus tried to pass by without being noticed. This "passing by" was like what is described in Exodus 34. Instead of being in the cleft of a rock, the disciples were in a boat, and glory was passing by. The God of glory walked with sinners and on water.

Later in Jesus's ministry, he took a few disciples with him on a mountain and unveiled his glory before them (Mark 9:2). This transfiguration was reminiscent of Old Testament encounters that Moses and Elijah had with God, so it was especially appropriate that these very prophets were there on the mountain with Jesus too (9:4; see Ex. 34, 1 Kings 19). Remembering that we were made to behold and reflect the glory of God, we can recognize that a scene like the transfiguration confirms God's plan to dwell among his people.

If the crowds during the days of Jesus's ministry had eyes to see and ears to hear, they would have rejoiced that ancient prophecies had been pulled together into the life of Jesus of Nazareth. His atoning work on the cross would have ensured the mercy of reconciliation. "For Christ also suffered once for sins," Peter wrote, "the righteous for the unrighteous, that he might bring us to God" (1 Pet. 3:18). Though all had sinned and fallen short of God's glory, God sent his Son that we might be united to him through faith.

Union with Christ is the gift of salvation to the unrighteous. Through the perfect work of the blessed Redeemer, we are brought to God, that we might be his people and he might be our God. Through union with Christ, "God restores believing image-bearers to participate in and reflect his glory. We are recipients of glory, are being transformed in glory and will one day be sharers of glory. Our salvation is from sin to glory."[5]

This Christian Life

While the Bible talks about people walking with God, it also talks about God walking with people. Christians affirm that God is transcendent, holy, and wholly other—yet he draws near. He is a God who communes. Though sin has disrupted the fellowship we were made

---

5   Christopher W. Morgan and Robert A. Peterson, *The Glory of God and Paul: Texts, Themes, and Theology*, New Studies in Biblical Theology 58 (Downers Grove, IL: IVP Academic, 2022), 40.

for, the Bible's story is about how God will bring us back to God. What would dwelling in sacred space accomplish if God were not with us?

The presence of God with his people is an assurance of his love and grace. Unlike the realms of Eden, the tabernacle, and the temple, our future with God will not be characterized by segmented degrees of access. We will behold the Lord. John wrote that when Christ appears, "we shall be like him, because we shall see him as he is" (1 John 3:2). We will behold and reflect God's glory, and as a result we will be glorified—*glorified*. You were made to experience this. C. S. Lewis is right: "We do not want merely to see beauty, though, God knows, even that is bounty enough. We want something else which can hardly be put into words—to be united with the beauty we see, to pass into it, to receive it into ourselves, to bathe in it, to become part of it."[6]

Your hardships will not derail or deny what is coming for you. Paul wrote that "the sufferings of this present time are not worth comparing with the glory that is to be revealed to us" (Rom. 8:18). The biblical authors want the hope of incomparable glory to shape our present discipleship. Hope is practical because thinking about future glory can give us a needed perspective about temporal trials. Hope helps us focus in the midst of afflictions, afflictions that might otherwise pull our focus entirely inward and earthward.

The end of the Bible emphasizes the God who dwells with his people. When John saw a vision of the new Jerusalem coming from heaven, he heard a voice from the throne: "Behold, the dwelling place of God is with man. He will dwell with them, and they will be his people, and God himself will be with them as their God" (Rev. 21:3). There, in that promise, the goal of Eden is complete. God will walk

---

6 C. S. Lewis, "The Weight of Glory," in *The Weight of Glory and Other Addresses* (1949; repr., New York: HarperCollins, 2001), 43.

among his people, and the new creation will be our dwelling place with him. On the cross, Jesus told one of the criminals, "Truly, I say to you, today you will be with me in paradise" (Luke 23:43). Those precious words were true not only for that man. Those words of Jesus will be reserved for every saint on every morning of our everlasting life in the age to come.

4

That Ancient Serpent

SOME OPENING SENTENCES DRAW YOU right into whatever is next. And some of these sentences even set you on edge, leaving you wondering if comedy or tragedy is around the bend. Genesis 3 begins like this: "Now the serpent was more crafty than any other beast of the field that the LORD God had made" (3:1). If that prompts concern or trepidation for what that might mean, we're reading those words correctly.

No one leaves Eden in order to find the arch nemesis of God's image bearers. The enemy comes to them. His appearance is sudden, his plans are menacing, and his words are poisonous. What can we know about this figure? How does later Scripture help us understand the serpent who enters sacred space with lies and snares?

A Rebel Ousted from Eden

The two Testaments speak with one voice that a being known as Satan or the devil opposes God and his people and seeks their ruin. Though the devil's origin is not narrated in the Bible, he is a created being because God alone is from everlasting to everlasting.[1] When readers overhear the devil's words with Eve in Genesis 3, he is already an adversary. So, while Genesis 3 does not report the fall of Satan, it does report his malicious work. It reveals his wicked heart, which twists and tempts. Jesus called him "a murderer from the beginning" and "the father of lies" (John 8:44).

When God created all things and called them good (Gen. 1:1–31), these created things included angels. So how did the devil become the devil? Sometimes interpreters bring Ezekiel 28 into this discussion. We should consider whether that chapter offers us any help regarding the devil's origin. In 28:12–15, the Lord says:

> You were the signet of perfection,
>> full of wisdom and perfect in beauty.
> You were in Eden, the garden of God;
>> every precious stone was your covering. . . .
> On the day that you were created
>> they were prepared.
> You were an anointed guardian cherub.
>> I placed you; you were on the holy mountain of God;
>> in the midst of the stones of fire you walked.

---

1 T. Desmond Alexander wrote of the devil: "While he is undoubtedly a most influential figure in the biblical meta-story, Scripture does not provide us with a detailed and comprehensive picture of him. We catch but occasional glimpses of this shadowy opponent. This should not surprise us. As divine revelation, the Bible exists to give us a deeper understanding of God. It is not designed to promote knowledge of the enemy, beyond what is necessary for comprehending the world in which we live and our own experience of it. Consequently, many questions remain unanswered when we collate what the Bible says about the devil or Satan." *From Eden to the New Jerusalem: An Introduction to Biblical Theology* (Grand Rapids, MI: Kregel Academic, 2008), 100.

You were blameless in your ways
from the day you were created,
till unrighteousness was found in you.

Looking at the content of what Ezekiel records, we find an angel (a "guardian cherub") who turned from wisdom to foolishness, from blamelessness to unrighteousness. First came pride, then came a fall. Yet this fall was a divine judgment. God says in Ezekiel 28:16–17:

In the abundance of your trade
you were filled with violence in your midst, and you sinned;
so I cast you as a profane thing from the mountain of God,
and I destroyed you, O guardian cherub,
from the midst of the stones of fire.
Your heart was proud because of your beauty;
you corrupted your wisdom for the sake of your splendor.
I cast you to the ground;
I exposed you before kings,
to feast their eyes on you.

The interpreter would be right to wonder how the rebellion of this cherub was tied to abundant trade (Ezek. 28:16) and how this cherub's judgment involved exposure before kings (28:17). What further complicates matters is the divine word to Ezekiel that precedes the address to this cast-down cherub. God said, "Son of man, raise a lamentation over the king of Tyre, and say to him . . ." (28:12).

The king of Tyre. But weren't we just reading about an ancient cherub from the days of Eden? As we look at what comes before Ezekiel 28:11–19, we will notice that this passage is in a series of oracles against nations that extends from Ezekiel 25 to 32. And among these oracles, Ezekiel 26–28 sets its sights upon Tyre. God will bring judgment. He will humble the proud.

The language in Ezekiel 28 is a taunt against the arrogant and lofty-minded king of Tyre. And this taunt is proclaimed with language evoking earlier folly and pride. Rather than only focusing on the king's current wickedness, the Lord's words depict the king in terms of an ancient rebel. But which rebel is in view? Some interpreters have argued that Satan is intended. We can see how this interpretation is plausible, since Satan is a rebel angel. Certainly the devil conducts himself with folly and pride. And we can imagine his prideful desire to be God or take the place of God (28:2, 6, 9).

Another possibility is that the taunting language evokes the ancient garden rebel known as Adam. The taunt says,

> You are but a man, and no god,
>> though you make your heart like the heart of a god. (Ezek.
>> 28:2)

The words to the human king, then, may be drawing upon—or may be a parody of—the garden king himself, Adam, who was a man. Other words in Ezekiel 28 could point to Adam. God said:

> You were the signet of perfection,
>> full of wisdom and perfect in beauty.
> You were in Eden, the garden of God. (28:12–13)

Adam's rebellion could be invoked.

You were blameless in your ways
from the day you were created,
till unrighteousness was found in you. (28:15)

His exile could be in view as well: "I cast you as a profane thing from the mountain of God" (28:16).

Since Adam had a priestly role in Eden, the words about certain stones in Ezekiel 28 are intriguing:

Every precious stone was your covering,
sardius, topaz, and diamond,
beryl, onyx, and jasper,
sapphire, emerald, and carbuncle. (28:13)

All these stones were on the breast piece of Israel's high priest (Ex. 28:17–21). Adam was a guardian-priest in Eden, and he had been made to walk in wisdom and beauty. Yet his heart turned to unrighteousness and thus became unclean. The outcome of his transgression was exile from the mountain of God.

Interpreters may not agree on whether Satan or Adam is in the background of the taunt in Ezekiel 28.[2] What we do *not* have in that chapter, though, is a clear narration of the devil's fall at some point before the events in Genesis 3.

---

2   Greg Beale says, "Whichever it is (Adam, I think), the king of Tyre's sin and judgment is seen primarily through the lens of the sin and judgment of the figure in Eden instead of his own particular sin, so that this most ancient figure becomes a representative of the king of Tyre, and the latter's sin and judgment is viewed as a kind of recapitulation of the primeval sin." *A New Testament Biblical Theology: The Unfolding of the Old Testament in the New* (Grand Rapids, MI: Baker Academic, 2011), 361.

Fallen from Heaven

Occasionally Bible readers will see part of Isaiah 14 as referring to Satan's rebellion. There is language of arrogance and self-exaltation, and God's response is to bring judgment and humiliation. The Lord says in 14:12–15:

> How you are fallen from heaven,
>> O Day Star, son of Dawn!
> How you are cut down to the ground,
>> you who laid the nations low!
> You said in your heart,
>> "I will ascend to heaven;
> above the stars of God
>> I will set my throne on high;
> I will sit on the mount of assembly
>> in the far reaches of the north;
> I will ascend above the heights of the clouds;
>> I will make myself like the Most High."
> But you are brought down to Sheol,
>> to the far reaches of the pit.

The name Satan doesn't appear in this passage, nor does the image of a snake or dragon. But the pride and god complex are similar to what we read from Ezekiel 28. The phrase "Day Star" (in Isa. 14:12) is translated "Lucifer" in the King James Version. This figure may be the one who can disguise himself as an angel of light (2 Cor. 11:14).

The above citation from Isaiah 14 began with verse 12. When we back up to verses near the beginning of the chapter, the context of

Isaiah 14 is clearer: "When the LORD has given you rest from your pain and turmoil and the hard service with which you were made to serve, you will take up this taunt against the king of Babylon" (14:3–4). Then the taunt begins, encompassing 14:12–15. The prophetic sights are on the king of Babylon. The people of God will taunt the one whom God will bring low. The presumed height will lead to a humiliating depth: the king's future is not the clouds but the pit.

Is Isaiah 14 about the king of Babylon, is it about the chief angelic rebel, or is it addressing Babylon's king with language invoking the ancient rebel Adam? The primary focus is a political ruler (see 14:4), and a historical divine judgment would undermine the self-assured king of Babylon. But the claims ascribed to this king (like "I will ascend above the heights of the clouds; / I will make myself like the Most High" in 14:14) reflect ancient roots. Not only are these claims rooted in self-exaltation and pride; they probably connect to an ancient Near Eastern world of Isaiah, where myths were known of gods vying for power and status yet being defeated.[3]

The taunt is mocking the Babylonian king. Thinking of himself as strong and exalted, the king will be revealed as weak and cast down. Spiritually speaking, what if we understood the king's arrogance as reflecting the self-exalting desires of his spiritual father? While Isaiah 14 is probably not about the initial rebellion of Satan, it still provides insight into the evil hunger for the status that God does not share.

Rebel Angels

The previous two sections addressed passages commonly used to describe the fall of Satan, though such an interpretation isn't obvious and

---

3   See Robert B. Chisholm, *Handbook on the Prophets* (Grand Rapids, MI: Baker Academic, 2002), 50–51.

is rather unlikely. We must also consider two passages in the New Testament that are sometimes thought to refer to Satan's "fall." For each of these passages, however, I'm going to suggest a different understanding.

In Jude's letter, he writes, "And the angels who did not stay within their own position of authority, but left their proper dwelling, he has kept in eternal chains under gloomy darkness until the judgment of the great day" (Jude 6). This is not a summary of the angelic rebellion that followed Satan's fall sometime after creation. This verse is part of a unit (Jude 5–7) that is referencing judgment stories early in the Pentateuch. Jude 5 refers to people who were judged after the exodus. Jude 6 refers to rebellious activity happening during the days of Noah (see 1 Pet. 3:18–20; 2 Pet. 2:4–10). And Jude 7 refers to the immorality of Sodom and Gomorrah.

In this unit of verses (Jude 5–7), and throughout his letter in general, Jude is drawing again and again from Old Testament accounts to illustrate his points. But there is no Old Testament narration of Satan's fall. Jude is recalling examples his readers would know from Old Testament books early in the Bible's storyline.

Another passage sometimes leveraged to address Satan's fall is from Revelation 12. In verse 4, John describes an action of the fierce dragon: "His tail swept down a third of the stars of heaven and cast them to the earth. And the dragon stood before the woman who was about to give birth, so that when she bore her child he might devour it." This dragon's action separates the stars (one-third from the other two-thirds), and some interpreters have considered this an angelic rebellion following Satan's fall.

In the context of what is happening in Revelation 12, however, verse 4 is part of an apocalyptic portrayal of the designs and ragings of the dragon collapsing before the victory of Christ. The second half of verse 4 has nothing to do with a pre–Genesis 3 fall of the devil.

Rather, it is about the dragon's malicious posture toward the Christ when he would be born. The seed of the woman would come to defeat the serpent-dragon. We should be hesitant to imply "the fall of Satan" from the apocalyptic imagery in Revelation 12. Such an early event doesn't fit the context of the chapter.

Revelation 12 does, however, provide a series of terms that confirm the identity of God's arch adversary. In verse 3 there is an image of a fierce dragon, and in verse 9 he is "that ancient serpent, who is called the devil and Satan, the deceiver of the whole world."

That Ancient Serpent

The last book of the Bible confirms that the serpent in the first book of the Bible is Satan, the accuser and deceiver of God's image bearers. And the earliest report of Satan's deceptive work is in Genesis 3. He was that ancient serpent from the days of Eden. No matter what you think of snakes in general, we can all agree that the description of the activity of the serpent in Genesis 3 is strange, extraordinary, even bewildering. What are we to make of this talking and tempting serpent?

Genesis 3 is the only narrative in Scripture where our adversary is a snake. But this created being wasn't made as a serpent. The presence of a speaking serpent in Genesis 3 means that Satan either took the form of a serpent or possessed a serpent. The text doesn't tell us which option we should believe, but either one may seem vexing to the reader. Why not simply appear as a mighty angel? Why not take a more intimidating or inviting or glorious form than a serpent?

Though no text after Genesis 3 depicts Satan as an animal in a narrative, we do read of demons possessing animals. In Mark 5, Jesus sends a legion of demons into a herd of pigs, and these pigs rush to their destruction off a steep bank and into the sea (5:9–13). Could the garden scene in Genesis 3 be the earliest record of something satanic possessing an animal? According to Luke 22:3, "Satan entered into Judas called Iscariot, who was of the number of the twelve." Clearly Satan can employ a vessel toward his twisted ends.

The usefulness of a serpent may connect to instructions God gave before the events of Genesis 3. God made the beasts of the earth "and everything that creeps on the ground according to its kind" (1:25), and he said, "Be fruitful and multiply and fill the earth and subdue it, and have dominion over the fish of the sea and over the birds of the heavens and over every living thing that moves on the earth" (1:28).

The snake was one of the creeping things. God's image bearers were to subdue what wasn't made in his image. Through a serpent, however, the evil one would subdue Adam and Eve, undermining God's design and created order. The serpent's promises laid the snare for disorder.[4] Rather than subduing the creeping thing, Adam and Eve were subdued by the creeping thing. This reversal was surely part of the appeal of Satan's strategy. God had made his creatures good (Gen. 1:31), and Satan's delight would be to mar this goodness.

Perhaps the extraordinary encounter with a speaking creature was also compelling to the woman. The other speaker she knew in Eden was her husband Adam, and he was a blessing and bore the image

---

4 As Andrew Naselli has observed: "*Serpent* is an umbrella term that includes both snakes and dragons. It's the big category. Snakes and dragons are kinds of serpents. . . . A serpent has two major strategies: *deceive* and *devour*. As a general rule, the form a serpent takes depends on its strategy. When a serpent in Scripture attempts to deceive, it's a snake. When a serpent attempts to devour, it's a dragon. Snakes deceive; dragons devour. Snakes tempt and lie; dragons attack and murder." *The Serpent and the Serpent Slayer*, Short Studies in Biblical Theology (Wheaton, IL: Crossway, 2020), 18; italics original.

of God. A speaking creature was probably alluring in both sight and sound. The only other occasion in Scripture where an animal speaks in a narrative is in Numbers 22, where Balaam is riding a donkey. The donkey rebukes Balaam, but those words come out because of a power beyond the animal (22:26–30). In Genesis 3:1, when a serpent speaks to the woman, the reader should assume that a power beyond the animal is at work—a power, in this case, that is dark and devilish.

The Adversary

The serpent was exceedingly crafty, the author says (Gen. 3:1). This claim is then proved by the conversation that followed. The snake was manipulative and deceptive. Satan convinced Eve that he was her ally when really he was her adversary. Now that's crafty! In Genesis 3, Eve trusts words that she thinks have her best interest at heart, yet the serpent means only to subvert and mislead.

The name Satan means "adversary," so whenever that name appears in Scripture, we are reminded that here is the foe—not friend—of God's image bearers. His adversarial ways continue after Genesis 3. While Satan is not a frequent character in the Old Testament, his wicked designs undergird the widespread deception and rebellion that the biblical authors narrate.

Satan's adversarial role is clear, for instance, in the book of Job. In Job 1:6, Satan comes with "the sons of God"—a phrase referring to angels—as they present themselves before the Lord. When the Lord speaks of the man Job, Satan insists that Job will curse God if Job's protection and possessions and health are gone (1:9–11; 2:4–5). The accusatory posture of Satan is reflected in the unsettling and afflictive accusations of Job's friends in the many chapters that follow. Job has an accuser, yes, but he also has an advocate—the Lord. Job knows that the Lord knows his integrity and faithfulness. Job knows that the Lord knows the truth, despite the caricatures and falsehoods his "friends" so confidently pronounce.

In the book of Zechariah, we read another example of Satan's accusatory work. The prophet Zechariah is ministering after many Israelites have returned from Babylonian exile, and this ministry includes recording the visions he has received. One of these visions involves the appearance of Satan: "Then he showed me Joshua the high priest standing before the angel of the LORD, and Satan standing at his right hand to accuse him" (3:1). This Joshua (different from the one who led the Israelites across the Jordan River centuries earlier) is a high priest and thus occupies a crucial role among the Israelite returnees. Yet even Israel's high priest is a sinner, and Satan stands ready to bring accusations against him.

But Satan cannot withstand the Lord's rebuke (Zech. 3:2). The Lord is sovereign over the evil one, just as Leviathan cannot withstand the Lord's hook and rope (Job 41:1–2).[5] Satan may be a mighty adversary, but he is not almighty. Satan may bring accusations to our minds about our real failings and guilt. What can mute the sound of these charges? Or, a better question, who can be our advocate against the deceiving and devouring ways of our adversary?

Tempter in the Wilderness

The message of the New Testament includes the discovery that Jesus was tempted yet was without sin. He was the spotless Lamb, bearing

---

5 The beginning of the book of Job features Satan by name, and clearly God is sovereign over him. Near the end of the book, the reader sees God's sovereignty over a mighty and untamable figure called Leviathan (Job 41). This penultimate chapter likely depicts Satan in a poetic and monstrous way. The subduing of Leviathan is the reader's hope that Satan cannot resist the hand and might of our sovereign God.

no moral blemish. The most famous scene of temptation in Jesus's life was before his public ministry began (Matt. 4:1–11; see also Mark 1:12–13; Luke 4:1–13). He was led by the Spirit into the wilderness "to be tempted by the devil" (Matt. 4:1).

When you think about temptation and the wilderness in Scripture, what comes to mind? In the Old Testament, the Israelites were tempted in the wilderness and faltered. Their murmuring and unbelief were on display, and the Lord judged them with forty years of wandering as many of them died (Num. 13–14). But in the New Testament, Jesus endured temptation in the wilderness and didn't falter. Israel was unfaithful; Jesus was faithful.

When we read about Jesus's wilderness temptation, that reminds us of Israel's. And when we read about Jesus's temptation by the devil, that reminds us of Eden. There is no report in the Old Testament wilderness journey that the tempter approached Moses or Aaron or Joshua. But Matthew tells us that "the tempter came" to Jesus and spoke (4:3). The appropriate background to Jesus's temptations, therefore, isn't *either* Eden *or* Israel's wilderness wandering—it's *both*. Jesus is the last Adam and true Israel. And the tempter who was at work during Old Testament history was also at work in the New Testament era.

While Satan aimed to twist truth and deceive the Son, Jesus held fast to the words of God (Matt. 4:4, 7, 10). "It is written" was the pattern of his reply. Jesus was the embodiment of wisdom, and his heart treasured the words of Scripture. There was no temptation clever enough or prolonged enough to ensnare him. He discerned every falsehood. The obedience of Jesus was crucial to the mission he would accomplish on the cross. If Jesus had sinned when tempted, he would have needed forgiveness and couldn't have been the source of atonement for others.

"Be gone, Satan!" Jesus told him (Matt. 4:10), and the devil left until a more opportune time (Luke 4:13). Yet, at no point prior or subsequent to this wilderness scene did the Son of God sin in his words, deeds, or heart. Unlike our fallen condition, the heart of Christ was the uncompromised center of righteous thoughts and holy affections and godly wisdom. Our adversary had met our advocate.

A Ruler and Prince

During his last week of ministry before the cross, Jesus alluded to something he would accomplish: "Now is the judgment of this world; now will the ruler of this world be cast out" (John 12:31). The fruits of Jesus's death on the cross would include victory over the world's "ruler," which referred to the devil.

Calling the devil a ruler isn't undermining God's sovereignty over all things. Jesus knew the influence and character and standing of the evil one. The apostle Paul called Satan "the god of this world" (2 Cor. 4:4) and "the prince of the power of the air" (Eph. 2:2). The devil is a leader and lover of darkness.

Even after the cross, Satan seeks the demise of God's people. He is like a raging dragon making war on the saints (Rev. 12:17). He is like a prowling lion seeking someone to devour (1 Pet. 5:8). While his accusations cannot condemn those who are in Christ, he hurls his charges like barbs and arrows, hoping to bring discouragement and distraction and despair. He remains a crafty tempter.

Paul says that Christians do not ultimately wrestle "against flesh and blood, but against the rulers, against the authorities, against the cosmic powers over this present darkness, against the spiritual forces of evil in the heavenly places" (Eph. 6:12). The reality of this warfare is the reason for Paul's command in Ephesians 6:11: "Put on the whole armor of God, that you may be able to stand against the schemes of the devil."

The devil had schemes in Eden, and he has schemes in your life. The writer James said, "Resist the devil, and he will flee from you" (4:7). The meaning of James's words is not about supernormal activity or exorcisms. It is about the ordinary Christian life. In the immediate context of 4:6, James is reminding his readers about the dangers of quarrels and the importance of submission to God (4:1–7). When we turn from fleshly impulses and reject sinful solutions to relational problems, we are resisting the devil. When we walk humbly with others, we diminish the devil's strategies to get a foothold in our lives and in our churches.

This Christian Life

The tragedy in Eden involved not only the sins of Adam and Eve but also the deceptive words of the serpent. This figure was their adversary and became ours as well. In order to understand the nature of temptation and the wicked schemes set against us, we must reflect on this ancient rebel. We must see how pride can form a devil from an angel. And as we persevere through the manifold sufferings and trials of life, our ultimate warfare is spiritual. We see the crafty serpent in Genesis 3:1, and we remember that we too are not above temptation.

Our minds can feel the crushing weight of guilt and shame. The evil one hurls his accusing darts, and they can land with profound effect. We wonder anew how God could love us, whether we're even saved, whether there's any hope. The words of the hymn "Before the Throne of God Above" are so relevant:

When Satan tempts me to despair
and tells me of the guilt within,

upward I look, and see him there
who made an end of all my sin.[6]

One chief scheme from the chief tempter would be to distract us so much with despair that the glories of Christ's victory seem dull or at least ineffective for us. Yet we can be encouraged by remembering that Jesus was the last Adam and true Israel, who faced the onslaught of the evil one's schemes and prevailed. We are conquerors in *the* conqueror. John expressed it this way:

> I write to you, young men,
>> because you are strong,
>> and the word of God abides in you,
>> and you have overcome the evil one. (1 John 2:14)

We don't always feel like overcomers. As we have a keen awareness of our sins, we may often feel like failures. So let us look upward. God has brought the devil low and raised Jesus up. Having no sin, Jesus took our sins upon himself and then satisfied the divine judgment for them. Now he intercedes for us in power and glory. Though Satan preys, Jesus prays. The Lord told Peter, "Simon, Simon, behold, Satan demanded to have you, that he might sift you like wheat, but I have prayed for you that your faith may not fail" (Luke 22:31–32). The intercession of Jesus is good news for the weary heart. Turn your eyes to the unfailing Christ who prays unfailing prayers.

---

6 Charitie Lees Bancroft, "Before the Throne of God Above" (1860), Hymnary. org.

5

Taking and Eating

BEFORE EVE WENT ASTRAY IN HER ACTION, she went astray in
her heart. That's the way it works for us too. Before a sinful deed is
chosen, it is considered, and it is considered because it seems desirable.
The dialogue in Genesis 3 reveals a wrong desire that manifested in
a particular deed. The crafty serpent stoked and facilitated the whole
deception. The power of the deception was how it connected to Eve's
desire. Our desires make us vulnerable because desires are powerful.

Though God made the man first and gave him the prohibition
about one specific tree (Gen. 2:7–8, 16–17), the serpent went not
to the man but to the woman. The conversation that followed had
epic consequences. Through the inspired account of Genesis 3,
we are being summoned as witnesses to what real people did in
a real place.

The Serpent's Question

If the reader recalls God's words to Adam about the trees in the garden,
then the serpent's opening question seems outrageous and misleading:
"Did God actually say, 'You shall not eat of any tree in the garden'?"

(Gen. 3:1). Who told the serpent such a thing? It's certainly not an accurate retelling of what God said.

God had told the man, "You may surely eat of every tree of the garden, but of the tree of the knowledge of good and evil you shall not eat, for in the day that you eat of it you shall surely die" (Gen. 2:16–17). When we see how pervasive God's allowance was, we can notice how pervasive the serpent's negation was. Instead of applying a "not" to the tree of the knowledge of good and evil, the serpent applied it to all the trees! Let's see things side by side:

Genesis 2:16	Genesis 3:1
God: "You may surely eat of every tree of the garden."	Serpent: "Did God actually say, 'You shall not eat of any tree in the garden'?"

The serpent's question was a deliberate distortion, but it was also a test. What would the woman remember? How did she understand God's prohibition? Would she agree with the falsehood or challenge it in some way? The serpent had fired a falsehood into the air, and he wanted the lie to land deep within her heart.

We're not told what the woman's initial reaction was to the presence and speech of this creature. Apparently this scene unfolded near the forbidden tree (see Gen. 3:6), but there is much we do not know. Was the woman curious or nervous? Was she suspicious, surprised, or nonchalant? How often had she come near to this tree before?

If God had made fruit-bearing trees throughout the garden and then forbidden his image bearers from eating any of the fruit, God would seem incredibly restrictive. A restrictive depiction of God, indeed, seems to be the point of the devil's question. He wanted to distort the character of God in order to strengthen the appeal of the temptation.

The devil's question in Genesis 3:1 depicts God as primarily closed-handed. He's the Creator of a lavish garden with fruitful trees, yet he refuses to extend them to his creatures for their enjoyment. He puts a stop sign in front of every trunk and an electric fence around the perimeter. If you need to eat, God is the kind of being who makes food and then deprives you of it. He's miserly, narrow, stingy.

If the serpent could make Eve wonder whether the goodness of God was a farce, his own alternative suggestion would be more compelling. An openhearted response to God would be reasonable and warranted if God himself was open-handed. But if God was actually a closefisted Creator who created goodness and yet withheld it, then his image bearers might have a more closed-hearted instinct toward him.

The serpent knew how important his strategy was of suggesting wrong assumptions about the character of God.

The Woman's Response

Eve disagreed with the serpent's words. She explained, "We may eat of the fruit of the trees in the garden" (Gen. 3:2), and this explanation corrected the serpent's caricature of divine words. While we are not told how Eve knew what she knew, it is possible that after God made her, he spoke the same information about the trees that Adam heard. It is also possible that Adam told her about the trees.

The next words from Eve have caused no small amount of reflection and commentary. Though the serpent applied God's restriction to all the trees in the garden, Eve said that God had prohibited only one tree: "But God said, 'You shall not eat of the fruit of the tree that is in the midst of the garden, neither shall you touch it, lest you die'"

(Gen. 3:3). While Eve mentioned "the tree" that is in the midst of the garden, we know there were *two* trees in the midst of the garden—the tree of life and the tree of the knowledge of good and evil (2:9). Given the prohibition and consequence that she recounted, the second tree was clearly meant. God had given no prohibition against the tree of life.

Let's isolate four ideas from Eve's response. First, there was a tree in the midst of the garden. Second, God said they must not eat the fruit of this tree. Third, God said they must not even touch the tree. Fourth, death was the consequence for doing what God prohibited. How many of these ideas are rooted in what we've learned before Genesis 3? There was a tree in the midst of the garden (2:9). God said not to eat from it and that the penalty for eating from the tree would be death (2:17). Keeping count, three out of four claims are from Genesis 2. What about her words that they were not supposed to touch the tree? There's no record of God saying that in Genesis 2. Let's look at things side by side once more:

Genesis 2:17	Genesis 3:3
God: "But of the tree of the knowledge of good and evil you shall not eat, for in the day that you eat of it you shall surely die."	Eve: "But God said, 'You shall not eat of the fruit of the tree that is in the midst of the garden, neither shall you touch it, lest you die.'"

A common way of understanding Eve's phrase "neither shall you touch it" is that she has added to what God said. And this may be what happened. She may have elevated her own words or practice to the same tier as God's command, similar to the religious leaders in Jesus's day who treated their manmade traditions with the authority of the law of Moses. If "neither shall you touch it" came not from God but from Eve, did it come from Eve first or from Adam? In other words, if "neither shall you touch it" is an error, did the error start in Eve's mind, or was she merely recounting what Adam told her? The short answer: we don't know.

A different way of understanding Eve's words is that they were not a wrong addition from her mind or Adam's. Instead, "neither shall you touch it" would represent additional revelation (which Gen. 2 has not reported) or at least an acceptable summary of what God expected. After all, if someone went to the forbidden tree to eat the fruit, he or she would first have to touch the fruit.

If Eve claimed that God said something he didn't say, she would be misrepresenting his words, and that would be wrong. If she elevated her own idea of obedience—"neither shall you touch it"—to the level of divine command, that would be wrong. But I think we should be slow to charge her with error here. Scripture will often give us additional information in a later chapter that isn't introduced in an earlier chapter. Consider also that Eve has already corrected the serpent's distortion (Gen. 3:1–2), she knew of the forbidden tree (3:3), and she knew the penalty of death if they ate the fruit (3:3).

In later Scripture, no biblical author ever charges Eve with adding her own words to God's words. So, if that is indeed her error in Genesis 3:3, no subsequent biblical passage confirms it as such. The focus, instead, is on the fact that she was deceived: "And Adam was not deceived, but the woman was deceived and became a transgressor" (1 Tim. 2:14). If Eve erroneously put words in the mouth of God, surely that would have been transgression. Yet the Scripture tells us she became a transgressor after she was deceived.

How did Eve become deceived and then transgress? It happened because the serpent openly contradicted God and distorted his character. And she believed the serpentine lie.

The Serpent's Denial

The Bible reader is shocked by the serpent's reply because the warning of God had been clear: "for in the day that you eat of it you shall surely die" (Gen. 2:17). Yet the serpent—bold and shrewd, wicked and conniving—said to the woman: "You will not surely die. For God knows that when you eat of it your eyes will be opened, and you will be like God, knowing good and evil" (3:4–5).

The fork in the road was now clearer. Whom would the woman believe? God had said she would surely die, yet the serpent said she surely would not! Who was right? Adding another layer to the sinister contradiction, Satan offered an explanation for why God misled the woman. God promised a punishment that wouldn't actually happen, all because God wanted to keep something desirable from his creatures. Again, it's a character issue. God's words can't be trusted because his motive is selfish. He doesn't want you to be like him. He doesn't want you to know what he knows.

Knowing good and evil is wisdom, so the serpent was suggesting that Eve could be wise like God if she wanted. The serpent was willing to disclose this little tidbit even though the Lord was unwilling. He told her that God knew "your eyes will be opened" (Gen. 3:5). That's quite a claim, since the woman may have thought she already had quite an open-eyed view of things: living in Eden, married to Adam, communing with God, tasked with the responsibility of propagating image bearers. To suggest that her eyes weren't opened (or at least not opened in some desirable way) might have been aimed at provoking her, perplexing her, raising her curiosity.

The serpent's attacks on God's character were strategic. He depicted God as closed-handed, misleading, and selfish. Eve couldn't really trust that God had her best interest at heart. He was keeping things from her, trying to make sure that she and Adam didn't end up knowing what he knew. But the serpent, well, *he* would tell her the truth. He'd be the one looking out for her, sorting through the divine lies she'd heard and believed. She'd been abstaining in vain and should not worry anymore. God had promised death for disobedience, but it was just an empty threat.

The serpent's speech in Genesis 3 is sparse. There's his question (3:1), the contradiction of God's warning (3:4), and his claim about God's motive (3:5). The serpent essentially moves from "Did God actually say?" to "God didn't mean what he said" to "God doesn't have your best interest in mind anyway; he's only thinking of himself." Satan could not force her to eat. But the deception had occurred. The doubt had been planted. The snare had been set.

The Man's and Woman's Sin

There's a lot going on in Genesis 3:6. The trap springs with the woman's deliberation. "So when the woman saw that the tree was good for food, and that it was a delight to the eyes, and that the tree was to be desired to make one wise, she took of its fruit and ate." Her choice flowed out of her perception of the tree. It was "good for food," "a delight to the eyes," and "to be desired to make one wise."

We shouldn't assume that Eve didn't see the tree as delightful before her conversation with the serpent. And surely the tree was already desirable for becoming wise, since it was called the tree of "the knowledge of good and evil." But it's the evaluation that the tree was "good for food" that changes the tone of the scene. God had said not to eat from the tree, yet now the woman deemed the tree good for food. The serpent's deception stimulated her desire. Though she had refused to touch and eat, she now "took of its fruit and ate" (Gen. 3:6). Knowing that God had warned about death as a consequence, she trusted the serpent's words, which had basically called God a liar. By taking the fruit, she was calling God a liar too.

The woman seized what was not hers to take, assuming a prerogative that wasn't hers to claim. If permission to eat from the tree was ever voiced, it should have come from the Lord and in his perfect timing. Instead, she deemed the serpent's words as sufficient reason to ignore God's words. Exchanging the truth of God for a lie, Eve took and ate with the goal of becoming like God.

Genesis 3:6 is already a stunning verse because of what we've just witnessed, but there is more: "and she also gave some to her husband who was with her, and he ate." The impression is that there is an immediacy between what she did and what he did. He "was with her" at the forbidden tree. She gave him some fruit, and then his actions mimicked hers: he took and ate. How long was he at the tree before this moment? Did he overhear his wife's conversation with the serpent? If so, did the serpent's words have the same effect on him that they had on her?

The verse does not tell us about Adam's arrival or what, if anything, he heard. The impression, however, is that he was present when his wife ate, for then he took from her and ate as well. There's no hint of resistance or reluctance. He was the one who had heard the Lord speak the word of restriction and warning (see Gen. 2:17), yet he ate from the forbidden tree nevertheless. Perhaps he was emboldened to eat once he saw that his wife survived her bite. Had the serpent been right all along—they would not surely die?

Adam had received God's word but did not keep it. Adam had been tasked with guarding the sacred space from defilement, yet the serpent's lies and deception had done their toxic work. "But," says Matthew Harmon, "instead of ejecting the unholy serpent from the garden and remaining obedient to God's law, Adam not only permits the serpent to remain in God's sanctuary but joins with him in his uncleanness."[1] Adam had been called to subdue and rule, not be subdued by a creature bearing hostile intent. Called to be a faithful prophet, priest, and king, Adam failed.

"Then the eyes of both were opened," says the author (Gen. 3:7). They had drunk the lie and eaten the fruit. They had defied the Lord and disbelieved his word. They did what was right in their own eyes, despite the divine warning. Great was their fall.

Seeing and Desiring

The power of perception was at play in the actions of the woman and the man. Eve "saw that the tree was good for food" and "a delight to the eyes" (Gen. 3:6). She would not have reached for what repulsed her. The power of the temptation was in its attractiveness, and it was attractive because it seemed to resonate with what she desired: "the tree was to be desired to make one wise" (3:6). The serpent downplayed the consequence, and surely this only enhanced the attractiveness of what stood before her.

When we read about certain wicked acts in later scripture, we notice language of seeing and desiring. This pair—seeing and desiring—ultimately recalls the Genesis 3 transgression, the rebellion against God. The biblical authors, then, sometimes depict a wicked act with

---

1 Matthew S. Harmon, *Rebels and Exiles: A Biblical Theology of Sin and Restoration*, Essential Studies in Biblical Theology (Downers Grove, IL: IVP Academic, 2020), 12.

language that recalls the first rebellion. It's as if the garden transgression is repeated outside Eden over and over again.

Genesis 6 reports that when the human race was multiplying on the face of the earth, "the sons of God saw that the daughters of man were attractive. And they took as their wives any they chose" (6:1–2). Notice the clustering of ideas in such short space. The sons of God saw what seemed attractive, good, desirable, and they took what they desired. This biblical chapter is too close to Genesis 3 for such a cluster to be happenstance. The rebellion of the "sons of God" is meant to evoke the rebellion of our first image bearers.

Genesis 12 tells of Abram's wife, Sarai, being taken into Pharaoh's household. Why did that happen? The biblical author describes a situation with language reminiscent of Genesis 3:6. Some Egyptian men "saw that the woman was very beautiful. And when the princes of Pharaoh saw her, they praised her to Pharaoh. And the woman was taken into Pharaoh's house" (12:14–15). Put another way, the Egyptian men saw what was desirable, and they took what they desired.

Beyond Genesis, consider the heinous sin of David in 2 Samuel 11. David "saw from the roof a woman bathing; and the woman was very beautiful. . . . So David sent messengers and took her, and she came to him, and he lay with her" (11:2, 4). Given the mighty accomplishments of David's life before this, a reader can consider this wicked deed as David's fall. This king's fall is described with language reminding us of the garden, when an image bearer saw what was desirable and then took it.

These examples from Genesis and 2 Samuel are sufficient to show how Genesis 3:6 becomes a kind of template that surfaces afterward in various biblical stories. Perception is compelling. Desire is alluring.

We take what draws us. The deceptiveness of sin, of course, is that temptation shows the bait and hides the hook. Sin never presents itself honestly.

This Christian Life

Part of following Jesus in this life means fighting against temptation. Our first parents failed in the garden, and now our track record outside Eden is marked with failure. We all know what it is like to see what is desirable and then take it. And we know that sinking feeling of surprise and shame when sin—which appeared so promising, so appealing at the time—sank its hook in us.

As the author James described the process of temptation and sin, his words invoked the template from Eden. He said: "But each person is tempted when he is lured and enticed by his own desire. Then desire when it has conceived gives birth to sin, and sin when it is fully grown brings forth death" (1:14–15). We won't pursue wickedness that isn't appealing. Our temptations are considered such because they pull at our desires, and not everyone's desires are the same. James is clear that before sin is committed outwardly, there is an inward desire and deliberation. Even if the sin seems more instinctive than premeditated, our sinful actions are the overflow of our heart condition (Matt. 15:18–20).

Our need is to receive the embrace of our all-sufficient overcomer. The Lord Jesus is the one who faced temptation and didn't succumb. Though the hook was dangled before him, he discerned the truth behind every temptation, behind every lie. The arch deceiver could not succeed against the Holy Son of God.

Christian discipleship flows out of our union with Christ the victor. He never pursued what was forbidden and only did what was honorable. From his holy heart came holy desires, and flowing into his life were holy words and actions. God sent his Son into the world because, without his righteousness and atoning work, we would surely die. The first Adam failed as a prophet, priest, and king, and so would we.

Our hope must be in the last Adam—the prophet, priest, and king we needed. We can pray in his name,

Lead us not into temptation,
>   but deliver us from evil. (Matt. 6:13)

God will answer that prayer for Christ's people. The evil one will not prevail against them, for they worship their Redeemer, who looked to the cross with resolve and perseverance. On the night before his crucifixion, he sat with his disciples at a Last Supper. While they were eating, "he took bread, and after blessing it broke it and gave it to them" (Mark 14:22). Jesus would be broken and given to them. His death would mean their life.

Thomas Watson explains the profound connection between the words of Jesus at the Last Supper and the ancient temptation in Eden: "'Take, eat,' shows the wisdom of God, who restores us by the same means by which we fell. We fell by taking and eating the forbidden fruit, and we are recovering again by taking and eating Christ's flesh. We died by eating the tree of knowledge, and we live by eating the tree of life."[2] Christ is ours by faith and always. He gives himself as our daily bread. We take and eat—and we will surely live.

---

2   Thomas Watson, *The Ten Commandments* (Carlisle, PA: Banner of Truth, 1965), 225.

6

A Broken Covenant

IF SOMEONE ASKED YOU what happened in Genesis 3, how would you respond? Multiple answers are correct: "Adam and Eve rebelled." "The serpent deceived the woman." "That chapter is about the fall of man." All of these are accurate. Would it ever occur to you, though, to answer with covenant language, "Genesis 3 is the story of a broken covenant"?

Our understanding of Genesis 3 is enriched when we notice the covenantal overtones of what transpired. It's possible you have read that chapter without ever considering a context of covenant. The sections below will not argue that understanding Genesis 3 requires a covenant framework. But when this chapter from Genesis is considered in the sweep of Scripture, we will realize how a covenantal framework deepens our grasp of the tragedy it tells.

Word and Concept

Before we look at the evidence supporting a covenantal understanding of what happened in Genesis 3, we must acknowledge that the word *covenant* does not appear in that chapter (or in Gen. 1–2). This observation need not derail us, because the absence of a word does not mean the absence of the concept. It would be a logical error to reason, "If the text doesn't apply the word *covenant* to God's relationship with Adam, then we shouldn't either." A concept may be taught in a passage without a particular word being present.

Think about how we have associated the garden of Eden with sacred space. There's no place in Genesis 2 or 3 where Eden is called a sanctuary or a temple. The reason we can call the garden a sanctuary isn't that we find that word in those chapters. Eden is depicted as a sanctuary. Furthermore, later Scripture treats Eden as a sanctuary. If we are only looking for the presence of a word to affirm a certain teaching, we may be committing the word-concept fallacy. This fallacy says, "If the word isn't there, the concept isn't there."

Would you be surprised to learn that God's covenant with David isn't called a covenant in the very chapter where the Davidic promises are first given? In 2 Samuel 7, God promises that an offspring from David's line will occupy the throne and rule forever (7:12–13). You will search in vain for the word *covenant* in those promises. Yet we naturally use this term to speak of what God made with the king. We think of 2 Samuel 7 as the place where the Davidic covenant was formed. The concept of a covenant is taught there, and later scripture treats that chapter as a covenant too. For example, David himself called God's arrangement with him "an everlasting covenant" (2 Sam. 23:5). One of the psalmists called God's words to David in 2 Samuel 7 "the covenant with your servant" (Ps. 89:39). Biblical authors recognized the concept of covenant even if the term itself didn't initially appear. And once they discerned that the concept of covenant was present, they could designate it with the term.

What exactly is a covenant? The word first appears in Genesis 6:18 when God tells Noah, "But I will establish my covenant with you, and you shall come into the ark, you, your sons, your wife, and your sons' wives with you." In this story, and in subsequent ones using the word *covenant*, a relationship between parties is in view. God's relationship with Abraham, Israel, and David is treated with the term and the concept. To be in covenant, then, is not to have a loose or vague relationship. A formal arrangement is meant.

A covenant is a formal arrangement with commitments between parties. I'm tempted to say "formal divine arrangement," because God initiates the Old Testament covenants with Noah, Abraham, Israel, and David. But there are horizontal—not just vertical—covenants as well, like arrangements between nations or between individuals. If Assyria and Egypt form a treaty, they enter a national covenant together. If a man and woman exchange vows and get married, they enter a marriage covenant together.

Both horizontal and vertical covenants are formal arrangements with commitments between parties. When God initiates a covenant, it is a divine arrangement, and when God makes a formal arrangement with people, the arrangement consists of promises. Think of a covenant as a jar. A jar is a container, and not every container will have the same thing inside. The biblical covenants contain different promises, even though the covenants are still formal relationships with commitments between parties.

Now, what would lead us to think that God had a covenant with Adam, and what did this covenant contain?

The Covenant Name

In the beginning, God created all things (Gen. 1:1). The word translated "God" is Elohim, and this word is used throughout Genesis 1. Elohim is Creator, the one who brings something from nothing by his word. This God, the one and only and living God, rested on the seventh day from all he had made (2:1–3). After the creation account, a new section of text begins, which introduces Eden and its garden. The opening of this new section says,

> These are the generations
> of the heavens and the earth when they were created,
> in the day that the LORD God made the earth and the heavens. (2:4)

Did you notice the name? Not just Elohim. The "LORD God" made all things. When English translations use "LORD" in large and small caps, the original language has the name Yahweh. "The LORD" spoke to Noah (Gen. 7:1). "The LORD" spoke to Abram (12:1), to Isaac (26:24), and to Jacob (28:13). "The LORD" spoke to Moses (Ex. 3:7) and to Israel (20:1–2). These opening books of Scripture reveal God frequently relating to his people with the name Yahweh.

Genesis 2 and 3 feature "the LORD God" relating to Adam and Eve. "The LORD God" made the garden (2:8) and the man (2:7). "The LORD God" gave the prohibition about the tree of the knowledge of good and evil (2:16–17). "The LORD God" pursued the hiding couple in the garden (3:8), spoke to them (3:9–13), made garments of skins for them (3:21), and exiled them from Eden (3:22–24). Long before Yahweh made himself known to Abraham, Isaac, and Jacob, he made himself known to Adam and Eve.

When God relates to his people, he relates to them in covenant. The use of the divine name Yahweh supports the existence of a covenant with Adam. This feature alone isn't decisive, but it is part of a cumulative case. God was revealing himself to his image bearers, and they knew him in Genesis 2–3 as "the LORD," the "I AM" who later revealed himself to Moses as the covenant-making and covenant-keeping God.

Some Bible readers might object to a patriarchal (and pre-patriarchal) knowledge of Yahweh's name because of what God told Moses: "I appeared to Abraham, to Isaac, and to Jacob, as God Almighty, but by my name the LORD I did not make myself known to them" (Ex. 6:3). These words appear to deny a revelation of God as Yahweh to the patriarchs (and, by implication, to those before the patriarchs). The interpretive tension is due to the fact that the name Yahweh appears more than 150 times throughout the book of Genesis, both in narration and in the speech of biblical characters themselves. For example, Abraham said, "I have lifted my hand to the LORD, God Most High, Possessor of heaven and earth" (14:22). How should we understand God's claim in Exodus 6:3 in light of the many uses of Yahweh in Genesis?

One possibility is that Moses, who certainly knew God as Yahweh, wrote the Torah stories using Yahweh in Genesis to show that the God of the exodus was the God of creation as well. Another possibility is that the verses after Exodus 6:3 further expound God's claim, showing that there was a particular way God was revealing himself to Israel. God recounts that he established a covenant promising the land of Canaan (6:4). That language recalls part of God's promises to Abraham (Gen. 12:7). God tells Moses that the groaning of the people has reached him, and he is ready to act on his covenant promises (Ex. 6:5). God wants him to tell the Israelites:

I am the LORD, and I will bring you out from under the burdens of the Egyptians, and I will deliver you from slavery to them, and I will redeem you with an outstretched arm and with great acts of judgment. I will take you to be my people, and I will be your God, and you shall know that I am the LORD your God, who has brought you out from under the burdens of the Egyptians. (6:6–7)

These verses teach that God will make himself known to the Israelites as "the LORD" who redeems them. The patriarchs and those before them did not know Yahweh as the redeeming God, but the Israelites will.

Neither position seems completely satisfying. In the first possibility, Moses would be portraying the patriarchs—and others before them—as using Yahweh's name, while no such name usage actually occurred from their lips. In the second possibility, we would be assuming that the pre-exodus knowledge of Yahweh was deficient or lesser in some way. Keep in mind, however, that Jacob spoke of God who had shepherded and redeemed him (Gen. 48:15–16). Isaac knew of God's power over barrenness, not only because Isaac himself existed (after his mother had been barren) but also because Isaac married a barren woman (21:1–7; 25:21). Abraham had experienced the power and faithfulness of God in his own life. He had received covenant promises (15:7–21), he witnessed God's judgment upon the wicked (19:23–29), and his barren wife bore a son (21:2). Before these things, God had delivered Abraham and Sarah out of Egypt by pouring plagues upon Pharaoh's household (12:10–20). The Genesis narratives demonstrate the power, faithfulness, and delivering grace of God.

A more satisfying solution to God's claim in Exodus 6:3 is that our translations may be creating an unnecessary problem. The Lord's words to Moses at the end of 6:3 might be better translated and understood as a rhetorical question: "Did I not make myself known to them?"[1] In other words, God isn't saying he hadn't made himself known as Yahweh to the patriarchs. Rather he is calling Moses to recognize that the one who is coming to rescue Israel is the same God who made promises to Abraham, Isaac, and Jacob. The rhetorical question emphasizes continuity rather than saying something new and different.

The parallels are noticeable when Exodus 6:2–3 is set in an A-B-A'-B' arrangement:

A   I am Yahweh.

   B   I appeared to Abraham, to Isaac, and to Jacob, as God Almighty.

A'   And my name is Yahweh.

   B'   Did I not make myself known to them?

It is reasonable to believe that Adam and Eve knew God as Yahweh. They were in fellowship with the Creator of all things. He had formed them and befriended them. He dwelt with them in a covenant relationship.

Blessing and Warning

Ancient Near Eastern covenants contained incentives for promise keeping, and these incentives included consequences for violating the conditions of the covenant. When the Israelites entered a covenant with Yahweh at Mount Sinai, he promised them blessings if they kept his commandments but curses if they disregarded his law (see Lev. 26, Deut. 28). The Israelites had to choose, essentially, between life and death.

---

1   See Duane A. Garrett, *A Commentary on Exodus* (Grand Rapids, MI: Kregel Academic, 2013), 244–45, esp. note 150.

Covenant blessings and warnings were not a late reality in the life of God's people. We see these things at play in the garden of Eden. God had told Adam, "You may surely eat of every tree of the garden, but of the tree of the knowledge of good and evil you shall not eat, for in the day that you eat of it you shall surely die" (Gen. 2:16–17). The warning in verse 17 promises a consequence for disregarding God's command.

If the image bearers had a relationship with Yahweh, if they received blessings in their life with him, and if they heard warnings about what straying from his commands would lead to, then we're looking at the ingredients of a covenant. A covenant with conditions (or commandments) meant duties or obligations for the covenant recipients. And God's words in Genesis 2:17 imply a duty to keep his command. This duty is confirmed by the couple's exile from Eden at the end of Genesis 3. God sends them out because they did not do what they should have done. They were not to eat from the tree of the knowledge of good and evil, yet they set aside that prohibition.

As noted earlier, the forbidden tree was not the only tree in the midst of the garden. God had placed "the tree of life" there as well, and he did not bar the couple from this tree (Gen. 2:9). While there is no report that Adam and Eve had eaten from the tree of life, they may have. The promise of greater life was at least held out for them in the symbolism of the tree of life. When God created Adam, the man was not yet all that he could be or would be. The presence of the forbidden tree—and the explicit warning—may have been part of a probationary period, a period of testing before the Lord would grant the couple to eat from the tree of the knowledge of good and evil.

A probationary period would not have been punishment but refinement. Adam was not sinful, but he was given the opportunity to grow in his trust in the Lord, pressing onward in spiritual maturity and communion. At some unknown point, this period of testing would presumably end, and our first parents would be able to enjoy fruit from the tree of the knowledge of good and evil in God's timing and instruction. The probationary period would have been a demonstration of obedience, of learning trust and submission to God's will and ways.

The tree of life represented the promise and hope of an escalated state. Adam was not immortal, but such life was possible. The promise of life is an implication we can draw not only from the tree of life in the garden but also from the prohibition in Genesis 2:17. If violating God's command meant death, we can infer that keeping God's command meant life. Divine blessing was not just good food from the numerous trees. Increased spiritual strength, edification, and communion would result from submitting to God's good commands. In the garden of Eden, man would not live by fruit alone but by every word that came from the mouth of God.

The First and Last Adam

Adam was the first image bearer, and that fact matters for what happened next. God placed him in the garden of Eden to work it and keep it (Gen. 2:8, 15), he provided for him (2:16), and he gave a prohibition about the tree of the knowledge of good and evil (2:17). Adam gave names to birds and beasts (2:20), yet there was no suitable helpmate to be found among them. So the Lord made the woman from the man, both being image bearers who should faithfully reflect and represent the Lord (2:21–25; see also 1:27).

Though God created the man first, the serpent went to the woman with his strategy of deception. And though the woman ate from the tree before her husband, the Lord called for the man and said, "Where are you?" (Gen. 3:6, 9). Before exiling the couple from Eden, the Lord focused attention on the man: "Behold, the man has become like one of us in knowing good and evil" (3:22). Then we're told that "the LORD God sent him out from the garden of Eden to work the ground from which he was taken. He drove out the man, and at the east of the garden of Eden he placed the cherubim and a flaming sword that turned every way to guard the way to the tree of life" (3:23–24).

These observations from Genesis 2 and 3 together support the federal headship of Adam. The man was more than the first image bearer; he was the head of the human race. Given this headship, his responsibility carried with it the potential for profoundly devastating consequences. If Adam was sent out of Eden, we were sent out in him too. When Adam acted, he acted in our place. The impact of his decision, therefore, was far-reaching and ongoing. When Adam took and ate, we were in him taking and eating. His problem became our problem; his fall, our fall.

Subsequent Bible passages narrate our death in Adam. We see this because Adam and Eve's descendants are born outside Eden, live outside Eden, and die outside Eden. The subsequent biblical storyline shows us, then, that what happened in the garden happened to us all. The apostle Paul wrote that "in Adam all die" (1 Cor. 15:22). *In Adam.* The way to make sense of Paul's union language is that Adam was the federal head of humanity. We come into this world outside Eden and "in Adam." Paul says that "by a man came death" (15:21). We are born into a world of death and are on our way to death. All of this teaches us that when the Lord promised Adam that "in the day that you eat of it you shall surely die" (Gen. 2:17), "you" was referring to Adam *and* everyone in Adam.

What we need is a new federal head. If being "in Adam" brings condemnation and death, we need an agent of rescue and life. We need someone who can stand in our place and whose deeds can be reckoned to us. We need our humanity revived and our condition remedied. Who will heal our deep wounds and deliver us from the mire of our sin? We need a new Adam, a last Adam. If the first man failed, we need an Adam who will be faithful and whose faithfulness will impact the present and future of all who are united to him.

Paul says that Jesus is the "last Adam" (1 Cor. 15:45). Jesus is the "man of heaven" (15:48), and by grace we are born again in him and "shall also bear the image of the man of heaven" (15:49). Jesus is our new head, the leader and champion of the new humanity. These assumptions about Adam and Jesus are what make sense of Paul's reasoning in Romans 5:12–21. Paul taught that "sin came into the world through one man, and death through sin, and so death spread to all men because all sinned" (5:12). The "one man" was Adam, and his sin was the disobedience in the garden of Eden. When Paul said, "The wages of sin is death" (Rom. 6:23), he was faithfully reading and applying Genesis 2:17 to those whose spiritual head is Adam.

In Romans 5, Paul declares that the work of Christ has both remedied and surpassed the grievous nature of Adam's sin. The gracious work of Jesus is in view when Paul says: "But the free gift is not like the trespass. For if many died through one man's trespass, much more have the grace of God and the free gift by the grace of that one man Jesus Christ abounded for many" (5:15). Adam's trespass brought condemnation and death, but Jesus's righteousness brought justification and life (5:18).

A Covenant of Works

Particular words in Romans 5 further confirm that Adam was in a covenant with the Lord. Paul calls Adam's sin a "transgression" (5:14) and a "trespass" (5:18). This language fits the violation of covenant conditions. If there were duties to perform and boundaries not to cross, those elements signal a covenantal framework. Adam transgressed God's revealed law. A boundary had been drawn, yet Adam trespassed.

Long before the words of Paul depicted Adam as a covenant violator, the book of Hosea alluded to Adam's garden sin. The prophet Hosea was conveying the divine lament about the spiritual condition of the divided nation of Israel. The Lord said:

> What shall I do with you, O Ephraim?
>   What shall I do with you, O Judah?
> Your love is like a morning cloud,
>   like the dew that goes early away. (6:4)

The Israelites were living as an unfaithful people. They were in covenant with the Lord, yet they were covenant breakers. This notion is the background to the comment in Hosea 6:7:

> But like Adam they transgressed the covenant;
>   there they dealt faithlessly with me.

The Lord was displeased with Israel's covenant disobedience. And he compared them to the first covenant transgressor—*Adam*. While Adam was not in the same covenant as the Israelites at Mount Sinai, there are interesting resonances between Adam's covenant and theirs.

The Israelites were given God's commandments, and there would be blessing if they kept his commands. If they rejected God's law, there would be consequences that could lead to exile from the sacred space of the promised land. Israel was like a new Adam, bearing the oracles of God in a special place, and they would be exiled from blessing and life if they rejected God's ways and did what was right in their own eyes.

Among Isaiah's oracles, the prophet laments the languishing sinners on the earth, for sin has entranced them and the curse has devoured them. Isaiah says:

> The earth mourns and withers;
>> the world languishes and withers;
>> the highest people of the earth languish.
> The earth lies defiled
>> under its inhabitants;
> for they have transgressed the laws,
>> violated the statutes,
>> broken the everlasting covenant.
> Therefore a curse devours the earth,
>> and its inhabitants suffer for their guilt. (24:4–6)

There is a picture of vast disobedience. The earth is defiled because the people are defiled. God's everlasting covenant has been broken. Edward Young wrote:

> Those who have frustrated the eternal covenant are not merely the Jews but the world generally. The frustrating of the covenant is something universal. For this reason we may adopt the position

that the eternal covenant here spoken of designates the fact that God has given His Law and ordinances to Adam, and in Adam to all mankind.[2]

God's covenant with Adam has sometimes been called the "covenant of works." That phrasing is intended to capture the importance of obedience for Adam to enjoy life and communion with God in the garden. But the wording "covenant of works" can easily be misunderstood, especially if we read back into Genesis 3 the negative statements from Paul about works. Paul taught that no one is justified on the basis of his or her actions or law keeping (Gal. 2:16). When theologians teach that Adam was in a "covenant of works," they are not implying that Adam merited or earned his standing with God.

There is no indication that when the Lord made Adam and placed him in the garden to be surrounded by blessing and generosity and life, Adam had done anything to merit those things. God was not compelled by any external force to create or bless. God created creatures in order that he might love them and bless them. In Genesis 2, Adam becomes the recipient of divine generosity that he hasn't sought or earned. The chief end of Adam was to glorify God and enjoy him forever. Adam was created on the sixth day, after the Lord had formed the world and seas and land (Gen. 1:26–31). Mankind was

---

2 Edward J. Young, *The Book of Isaiah*, vol. 2, *Chapters 19–39* (Grand Rapids, MI: Eerdmans, 1969), 158. Meredith Kline addresses the idea that Isa. 24 and Hos. 6 clarify the presence of a covenant in Gen. 1–3: "Isaiah 24:5 and Hosea 6:7 have been suggested as instances of this. Although the meaning of both passages is disputed, the everlasting covenant of Isaiah 24:5 definitely appears to refer to the creational arrangements and Hosea 6:7 probably refers to Adam as the breaker of a covenant." *Kingdom Prologue: Genesis Foundations for a Covenantal Worldview* (Eugene, OR: Wipf and Stock, 2006), 14.

the crowning act of creation. The narration in Genesis 1 indicates that God had made a world habitable for his image bearers.

The idea of works in the "covenant of works" refers to Adam's responsibility to receive God's wise commands with obedient trust and delight. Adam's standing with God had been granted by God when God created him, so the covenant of works didn't teach that Adam needed to be justified by his obedience. His nature wasn't sinful, but perfect obedience was still required. He was positioned to learn obedience and grow in the fear of the Lord. Brandon Crowe comments: "The reward offered was not proportional to Adam's work; nor could Adam put God in his debt. Instead, it was God's sovereign, beneficent, covenantal design to offer Adam much more than he, a creature, could ever earn."[3]

The covenant of works was the arrangement in which Adam was to enjoy life with God, and the life he knew would be surpassed by greater life to come. According to Richard Barcellos, the covenant of works was "that divinely sanctioned commitment or relationship God imposed upon Adam, who was a sinless representative of mankind (or public person), an image-bearing son of God, conditioned upon his obedience, with a penalty for disobedience, all for the bettering of man's state."[4]

Yet Adam transgressed the covenant. He, our federal head, rebelled. Understanding this federal headship is crucial for grasping the surpassing and gracious character of Christ's person and work. The Lord

3 Brandon D. Crowe, *The Path of Faith: A Biblical Theology of Covenant and Law*, Essential Studies in Biblical Theology (Downers Grove, IL: IVP Academic, 2021), 13.
4 Richard C. Barcellos, *The Covenant of Works: Its Confessional and Scriptural Basis*, Recovering Our Confessional Heritage 3 (Palmdale, CA: RBAP, 2016), 67.

Jesus, who brought new creation life and blessing, kept God's law in his heart and in his life. His way was pure. He was without sin. He grew in favor with God and man, learning obedience and delighting in divine wisdom. According to the author of Hebrews: "Although he was a son, he learned obedience through what he suffered. And being made perfect, he became the source of eternal salvation to all who obey him" (Heb. 5:8–9).

This Christian Life

Truly God and truly man, Jesus was not a transgressor like the first Adam. Our hope is the perfect righteousness of Jesus, which is credited to us sinners, whose standing without it would be condemnation. The gospel is good news because it proclaims Christ's substitutionary death, which flowed from his substitutionary life. Jesus lived the life we should have lived but couldn't have lived. Theologians refer to Christ's earthly obedience as his active obedience, which secures and demonstrates his role as our new federal head.

Union with Christ means we are no longer in Adam. We are now in Christ through faith. With the open hands of faith, we have received God's gracious provision of rescue in his Son. The disciple's whole life is the outgrowth of this new and inseverable union. We have been crucified with Christ and raised with Christ. Adam was "a type of the one who was to come" (Rom. 5:14), but their corresponding acts are contrasts. Adam broke God's law, while Christ kept God's law. And the new covenant that Christ established is a covenant that cannot be undermined, corrupted, or nullified. Life in the new covenant is life in Christ, and life in Christ means the tree of life is ours forever.

Discerning the covenantal frame for Adam's actions is important for the doctrine of justification. As Adam's actions impact all those in him, Christ's actions impact all those in him. Because of the perfect obedience and substitutionary death of Christ, we can be assured of our standing with Christ, for we are as secure before God as is the Son himself. The covenant of works provides a helpful background for us to appreciate the surpassing glory and grace of the cross. Through his body and blood, a new covenant was formed. Christ was broken for our sake that our union with him might be unbreakable.

7

Afraid and Ashamed

AFTER THE FIRST MAN AND WOMAN SINNED against the Lord, they went into hiding, and we went with them. Our sin has driven us to the trees because we are afraid. Our sense of shame has left us vulnerable, unsure. People respond to their fallen condition differently, some living under the crushing and unrelenting weight of their iniquity, others emerging from the trees with a fresh sense of confidence and shamelessness because of how they covered themselves.

What is clear is that fear and shame have come into our lives with our sin. There is always the danger of growing numb, leaving our consciences desensitized to wicked thoughts and deeds. When we reflect on the behavior of our first parents as they responded to what they had done, we can learn about our own hearts. When we notice their efforts at covering their shame, we will recognize the instincts that lurk within us. And when we listen to the blame shifting from their lips, we will hear its echoes in what we say to ourselves and others.

Fig-Leaf Coverings

Something had changed. The atmosphere seemed different now. With opened eyes, Adam and Eve "knew that they were naked. And they sewed fig leaves together and made themselves loincloths" (Gen. 3:7). They knew good and evil in an experiential sense—they had done what was evil. Eating the tree, for them, did not bring mature wisdom and discernment. Their eating showed their folly.

Their knowledge felt like shame, and the action they took next was an attempt to cover their shame. Earlier in Genesis, the biblical author told us, "And the man and his wife were both naked and were not ashamed" (2:25). We need this verse in mind when we watch the couple's response in 3:7. Their nakedness had once been an indicator of their innocence, their vulnerability mixed with intimacy. They were safe, in covenant, and blessed.

Once "the eyes of both were opened" (Gen. 3:7), their perception of each other was no longer marked by innocence and security. They knew internally about good and evil in a way that had first sounded appealing (see 3:6) but proved devastating (3:7). Though the serpent had said they would be like God, they responded very unlike God, pulling leaves and trying to sew them together. They looked altogether undivine.

Their sinful deed could not be undone, but perhaps they thought their shame seemed so obvious, *too* obvious. Their vulnerability now connoted insecurity. They "made themselves loincloths" out of fig leaves. That brief description does not imply a sixty-second act. Picture their distress and angst. They're looking around and sensing things foreign and unwanted. Fig leaves are available. Are these leaves from the tree of the knowledge of good and evil? Perhaps, since the couple have just eaten fruit from this tree in the midst of the garden (Gen. 3:7). Suddenly they feel shame and act to cover themselves.

If the leaves were from the forbidden tree just as the fruit had been, then interpreters can see that the leaves were no more help for them than the fruit itself. Sewing loincloths would take some time, but the covering was no remedy. And who were they covering for? One another, as husband and wife? There were no other image bearers in the garden. The making of loincloths signaled a change in the man and woman's mindset. If you're sewing a loincloth, you're not throwing it away a few hours later. This is your clothing, at least for now. As far as they were concerned, dwelling in the garden would involve less openness. They sewed loincloths because things weren't going to be like before.

Tree Coverings

At some point, "they heard the sound of the LORD God walking in the garden in the cool of the day" (Gen. 3:8). This sound was one they knew, for they had walked with God and God with them. They had enjoyed the fellowship of his presence and the delight of being his. They had exulted in his love and freely received his blessings.

But this time would not be like the others. When they heard the Lord, "the man and his wife hid themselves from the presence of the LORD God among the trees of the garden" (Gen. 3:8). Loincloths were inadequate, for the couple needed more than their nakedness covered. They wanted their selves removed from view. This removal was what the loincloths stood for anyway. Faced with the shame of their sin, the man and woman wanted to hide from God.

Readers can note, first of all, the absurdity of hiding from God. Image bearers can hide nothing from the God who knows all and sees all. What might be successfully suppressed from the sight of another person is still exposed before the gaze of God. Hiding among the trees didn't demonstrate theological sophistication, but it certainly demonstrated their instincts of fear. Note, second, that the couple hid among the trees God had given in Genesis 2 as a blessing. Verse 9 says, "The LORD God made to spring up every tree that is pleasant to the sight and good for food." Afterward God told the man, "You may surely eat of every tree of the garden" (2:16). The trees of the garden were fruitful symbols of God's generous hand. He had made man and woman in his image and then provided for them too. These signs of blessing became coverings. The provision from God's hand had become shelter from God's presence.

The Lord, who had made the man and commanded the man and commissioned the man, now questioned the man: "Where are you?" (Gen. 3:9). The "you" is singular, referring to Adam. Though Eve had eaten the fruit first and handed some to her husband (3:6), the Lord called for him. Adam was the federal head, the representative of humanity. When Adam acted, he wasn't acting for himself alone. When Adam sinned, he didn't experience ramifications for himself alone.

The question ("Where are you?") was a question Adam needed to ask himself. The Lord wasn't missing information. He knew exactly where Adam was because, well, he is the Lord. But it was important for Adam to voice the fear and shame he was feeling in the garden. The serpent's opening question ("Did God actually say . . . ?") was meant to draw the woman—and ultimately the couple—into the dark. Despite the transgression, the Lord God came walking in the garden in the cool of the day, and his opening question was meant to draw the man—and ultimately the couple—into the light. The question was meant to draw Adam out of hiding. His sin produced shame, and neither loincloths nor trees could conceal the transgressor. Adam needed to own, not deny, what had happened. It was time to step into the light.

Shame and Blame

Drawn into conversation with the Lord by a question ("Where are you?"), Adam couldn't give a simple answer. He didn't say, "I'm in the trees with my wife." He explained that his location was due to fear, and the fear was due to the sound of the Lord: "I heard the sound of you in the garden, and I was afraid, because I was naked, and I hid myself" (Gen. 3:10).

An immediate effect of sin in Adam's heart was that God's presence was unwelcomed. Sinners have an impulse to put distance between them and whatever prompts the guilt and shame of their transgressions. When readers listen to Adam's words in Genesis 3:10, we're hearing the stiff-armed response of a man trying to barricade himself. The Holy One has drawn near, so Adam wants to go far, but no distance will be far enough. Transparency repels him, but his transgression faces the "problem" of divine omniscience and omnipresence.

Adam's answer says he was afraid, "because I was naked" (Gen. 3:10). This reference to nakedness explains the Lord's response: "Who told you that you were naked? Have you eaten of the tree of which I commanded you not to eat?" (3:11). These two questions are piercing. Where had Adam gotten the information about nakedness? If he was afraid and hid because he was naked, how did shame become associated with his nakedness? In Genesis 2:25, the man and his wife were naked and *unashamed*. Now they were naked and ashamed.

The answer to the Lord's first question in Genesis 3:11, of course, is that no one had told Adam he was naked: "Then the eyes of both were opened, and they knew that they were naked" (3:7). A realization had taken place. Adam had to deal with the truth that his nakedness—and its accompanying shame—was his own realization, not information from the outside that he came to believe.

God's next question was "Have you eaten of the tree of which I commanded you not to eat?" Perhaps the reader expects the hiding man to say, "No, I didn't eat from that tree!" Adam didn't deny it though. Denial would have been a foolish response anyway, since there's no point in denying what God already knows. Furthermore, Adam couldn't have pled ignorance about the forbidden tree. God had directly commanded him not to eat from it (Gen. 2:17).

While denial or a plea of ignorance would have been inadequate, Adam's actual response is stunning, bold, and outrageous: "The woman whom you gave to be with me, she gave me fruit of the tree, and I ate" (Gen. 3:12). Adam didn't want the light on him, so he immediately pushed his wife's transgression into the light as well. Adam is the first blame shifter. He could have simply said, "I ate." But he prefaced his admission: "The woman whom you gave to be with me, she gave me fruit of the tree." His qualification was longer than his confession! Though it was technically true that the woman gave Adam the fruit, that did not absolve his responsibility. In fact, we can understand Adam's reply here to be a kind of *evasion* of responsibility. "She gave me fruit," he said, as if he hadn't been in covenant with God and bearing covenant duties of submission to God's good and wise law. Adam had been "with her" when she ate, and there's no indication that he tried to intervene. Had he heard the serpent's twisted words and contradiction of God's warning (3:1, 4–5)?

God had called to Adam, and Adam pointed to Eve. As we look closely at Adam's response, we'll also notice that he invoked what God did: "The woman *whom you gave to be with me*, she gave me fruit of the tree, and I ate" (Gen. 3:12). Adam was merely accepting what others were giving him. The fruit came to Adam from Eve, and Eve came to Adam from God. Genesis 2 had ended with the presentation of Eve to Adam. The Lord God "brought her to the man" (2:22), and Adam made a poetic declaration of his union with her (2:23). Now in Genesis 3 we find Adam handling his shame by shaming her. Failing to lead and love well, he acted as an accuser. His meager confession was buried under blame shifting. His response was tantamount to saying to God, "Eve was the reason I had the fruit, and you're the reason I had Eve."

The Lord then turned his words to the woman: "What is this that you have done?" (Gen. 3:13). This question opened the opportunity for humble confession of the transgression. Eve's answer did arrive at "and I ate," but not before she pointed her finger as well. "The serpent deceived me," she said, "and I ate" (3:13). Her words to the serpent in Genesis 3:2–3 made clear that she knew of God's command. The deception of the serpent was successful, but not because Eve lacked necessary information. She knew the prohibition and the penalty. In spite of what Eve knew, she believed Satan's lies instead—lies that twisted God's words, denied God's warning, and impugned God's motives.

Defiled and Distant

When we watch Adam and Eve deal with their shame and guilt, we can see ourselves in them as well. To the sinner, utter divine holiness is not a welcomed reality. Having fallen short of glory, we shirk back from righteousness. We pull away from purity. The light of holiness is uncomfortable, blinding, searing.

Outside Eden, image bearers have hearts defiled by sin. We need this uncomfortable truth. Our joy in Christ, the sin bearer, depends on it. Mark Jones has written, "Other than knowing God, your greatest advocate, nothing else in this world is more important than knowing sin, your greatest enemy. . . . A distorted, weak view of sin will lead to a disfigured, anemic, and unproductive theology."[1]

We can follow the biblical instruction about sin, through both description and prescription, as we track with the generations after Eden. The lives of the Israelites were filled with regulations and ceremonies that reminded them of uncleanness. Certain foods could make the Israelites ritually unclean (Lev. 11). Certain emissions could leave men and women ritually unclean for spans of time (Lev. 12, 15). The fallen world was marked by moral defilement, and this spiritual truth was woven into the symbols of tabernacle and ceremonial regulations. The lives of the Israelites had constant reminders that they needed the merciful and cleansing power of God upon their hearts. Uncleanness was not merely an outward problem.

Jesus taught that what comes out of a person's heart is what makes him or her unclean (Matt. 15:10–20). He wasn't addressing a recent development in the human condition. The words of Jesus were true for image bearers after the events of Genesis 3. Lies are believed in the heart, sins are contemplated in the heart, and deeds are performed out of the overflow of the heart.

In the light of God's commandments, we are rightly designated as transgressors. We have trespassed the boundaries of goodness and righteousness, and we are guilty. We cannot rescue ourselves from our state of shame. We are unclean, and we cannot make ourselves clean again. The defilement is too deep, too intractable. Our spiritual state is not like Adam's pre-sin state. He was able to not sin. After Adam, sinners possess a corrupted nature. Our corruption affects our desires

---

1   Mark Jones, *Knowing Sin: Seeing a Neglected Doctrine through the Eyes of the Puritans* (Chicago: Moody Publishers, 2022), 13.

and is expressed by them. We possess a genuine will, yet the decisions we make are according to a fallen nature. Our loves are twisted.

Another way to describe the sinner's condition is that we are born "in Adam." David's questions and answers in Psalm 15 leave us looking for a rescue outside ourselves. He says:

> O LORD, who shall sojourn in your tent?
>> Who shall dwell on your holy hill?
> He who walks blamelessly and does what is right
>> and speaks truth in his heart. (15:1–2)

As we are, we cannot dwell with God as he is. And so we hide. We hide behind work, behind money, behind possessions, behind reputation. We are the unrighteous trying to cover ourselves with loincloths and among the trees. We are afraid. We are afraid to be known, to be vulnerable, to shine light in the dark places. We have believed falsehoods about God and God's ways.

Distance from God may feel safe, but that's only a delusion. There's no concealment from the all-seeing one. David said:

> Where shall I go from your Spirit?
>> Or where shall I flee from your presence?
> If I ascend to heaven, you are there!
>> If I make my bed in Sheol, you are there! (Ps. 139:7–8)

Let God's question to Adam draw us out: "Where are you?"

As we encounter God through the truth of his word, and especially the gospel, we need to respond differently than Adam and Eve. Don't point fingers. Don't deflect. In the mirror of God's wise commands, we must see that we have all sinned and fall short of the glory of God. The good news is that after Adam and Eve sinned, God came to them. When you hear the good news of what God has done in Christ, the God of the garden is drawing near to you.

Facing Our Sinful Selves

We cannot fully comprehend the horror of our spiritual condition, and our spiritual condition is the reason why. Our sin prevents us from seeing the scope and depth of our sin. But as the nature of our condition becomes clearer, we might recoil at what we do see. Think of the prophet Isaiah when he had a vision of the Lord. He saw the glorious presence of God, which was hailed by angelic voices. The seraphim cried out,

> Holy, holy, holy is the LORD of hosts;
> the whole earth is full of his glory! (Isa. 6:3)

In the presence of glory and holiness, Isaiah had a keen sense of his own sin. "Woe is me!" he declared. "For I am lost; for I am a man of unclean lips, and I dwell in the midst of a people of unclean lips; for my eyes have seen the King, the LORD of hosts!" (6:5). The prophet's recognition and confession are refreshing. He doesn't sound like Adam. Isaiah knew God's holiness, so he had a better understanding of his guilt and desperate condition. The response of the Lord is seen in the action of a seraph, who touched Isaiah's lips with a burning coal and said, "Behold, this has touched your lips; your guilt is taken away, and your sin atoned for" (6:7).

Loincloths and tree coverings cannot atone for sin. We need confession and forgiveness. We offer the former, and God provides the latter. A true sense of sin confronts us with our unworthiness to receive mercy, yet the beauty of mercy is that it is undeserved. To mix metaphors, our loincloths are just filthy rags (Gen. 3:7; Isa. 64:6). We need our guilt removed. We need our sins covered, and only God can cover the deeds we have done against him. Sin, says Mark Jones, is "the soul's disease, blinding the mind, hardening the heart, disordering the will, stealing strength, and dampening the affections."[2] We are helpless before God, and our only hope is God.

Our admission could sound like the words of Peter. In Luke 5, Jesus performs a miracle from a boat, and the fishermen witness an extraordinary catch of fish (5:6–7). In the presence of such power and wonder, Peter immediately senses his own unworthiness. They have never met anyone like Jesus. The holy, holy, holy God is walking among sinners. Peter says, "Depart from me, for I am a sinful man, O Lord" (5:8).

Peter's instinct is like Adam's: in the presence of such greatness and glory, create some distance. But the sinfulness of Peter is not new information to Jesus. He knows Peter's condition before getting into the boat! Peter knows he is a sinner, but that doesn't bring the scene to an end; sinners are the people Jesus came for. Peter wants to put up some distance, but Jesus has already crossed the distance to come to him. Jesus tells Peter words that calm the soul of anxious and terrified sinners: "Do not be afraid" (Luke 5:10). Jesus knows the fear in Peter's heart, so he addresses it. In the presence of unrivaled glory and holiness, fear seems reasonable. But Peter's fear isn't a reason to distance himself, and his sin isn't a reason to send Jesus away.

2   Jones, *Knowing Sin*, 39.

Jesus has come to call sinners out of the darkness and into the light. He came—and still comes—for the hiding and the fearful, the ashamed and the sinful. Do not be afraid. The rescuing grace of God has stepped into the boat.

This Christian Life

The promise of the new covenant is a deep cleansing of the heart.

> I will sprinkle clean water on you, and you shall be clean from all your uncleannesses, and from all your idols I will cleanse you. And I will give you a new heart, and a new spirit I will put within you. And I will remove the heart of stone from your flesh and give you a heart of flesh. (Ezek. 36:25–26)

Do you see the truth of your defilement? There is cleansing in Christ. Do you understand your hardness of heart? There is a new heart in Christ. The new covenant consists of sinners who are now united to Jesus by grace through faith. They have forsaken the loincloths and tree coverings. They have come out of hiding in order to find a new refuge. The work of Jesus is the burning coal to purify us.

Because Christians have not experienced the resurrection of the body and the fullness of God's sanctifying work, we are still short of glory. Nevertheless, we are free in him from the penalty and power of our transgressions. We can walk in honesty, confessing our sins and rejoicing in the finished work of Christ on our behalf. It would be futile to err in the ways that John wrote about in his first letter: "If we say we have no sin, we deceive ourselves, and the truth is not in us" (1 John 1:8). Or, "If we say we have not sinned, we make him a liar, and his word is not in us" (1:10). Let's not be deceived, and let's not call God a liar. We have sinned and have sin.

The believer's answer to the question "Where are you?" is different from the Genesis 3 context. We now answer "Where are you?" by saying, "I am in Christ." My covering comes not from fig leaves but from the old rugged cross. Our refuge is not among the trees but under *the* tree. The cross has become the tree of life for sinners. It is there that our atonement was accomplished.

We may feel tempted to say to Jesus, "Depart from me," but he is saying to us, "Come to me." As the light of God's word reveals our transgressions and we sense greater depths of our shame, we may feel overwhelmed. But your sin does not overwhelm Christ. If you say to him, "I am afraid, for I cannot bear my sin," he will say to you, "Fear not, for I already bore your sin." Don't walk—*flee*—to the refuge of his mercy tree. The very reasons you think he should depart are the very reasons he tells you to come.

8

Salvation through Judgment

IT IS NORMAL TO SEE GENESIS 3 as a chapter full of despairing things. Any reader who sees it that way has good reasons. There is a deceiving serpent who succeeds in his ploy. There is a woman who turns from God's command and believes lies. There is a man who receives and eats what God has prohibited. There is shame and fear. There is concealing and blame shifting. But that's not all there is.

Hope shines bright against the dark. And into the darkness, God speaks a promise of hope. This promise will mean judgment for the serpent, but it will mean deliverance for sinners. The defeat in the garden will be followed by a victory. The serpent's craftiness will be outwitted. The serpent learns that his judgment is sure, and through this judgment, salvation will be accomplished.

Pronouncing a Curse

Starting in Genesis 3:14, the Lord speaks a series of consequences to those in the garden. And the order in the following verses inverts the order of references to the characters in the preceding verses. When the Lord came to the garden, he addressed the man, the man's response mentioned the woman, and the woman's response mentioned the serpent (3:9, 12, 13). God's words in 3:14–19 address these figures in reverse order: first the serpent (3:14–15), then the woman (3:16), and lastly the man (3:17–19).

Apparently after tempting Eve, the serpent remained in the garden. And after Eve said, "The serpent deceived me, and I ate" (Gen. 3:13), the Lord directed his next words to the crafty creeping thing. He told the serpent:

> Because you have done this,
>> cursed are you above all livestock
>> and above all beasts of the field;
> on your belly you shall go,
>> and dust you shall eat
>> all the days of your life.
> I will put enmity between you and the woman,
>> and between your offspring and her offspring;
> he shall bruise your head,
>> and you shall bruise his heel.

The action of the serpent warranted divine judgment ("Because you have done this"). In a world brimming with blessing, God now pronounced a curse. The pronouncement is shocking to the reader of Genesis 1–3, because God had blessed (1:22) and blessed (1:28) and blessed (2:3) what he had made. A curse was the opposite of flourishing. It was a death sentence, a promise of demise. Because the devil had come to the woman as a creeping creature, the Lord's curse upon the evil one came in corresponding language. There was a surpassing quality of the judgment ("above all livestock and above all beasts of the field"). The one who subjected the woman and then the man would be subjected. The humiliating nature of the judgment is clear: "on your belly you shall go, and dust you shall eat." Eating dust was an image of defeat. And this defeat wouldn't be temporary. The curse would be ongoing upon the serpent: "all the days of your life."

By cursing the serpent with these words, God promised that the enemy of God's people would face humiliation and condemnation. The images in Genesis 3:14 influenced later biblical texts. In Psalm 72, the psalmist is speaking of the future Davidic king in words that evoke an enemy with its face in the dirt. Of the coming king, the psalmist writes:

> May he have dominion from sea to sea,
> and from the River to the ends of the earth!
> May desert tribes bow down before him,
> and his enemies lick the dust! (72:8–9)

Similar language appears in Isaiah:

> Kings shall be your foster fathers,
> and their queens your nursing mothers.
> With their faces to the ground they shall bow down to you,
> and lick the dust of your feet.
> Then you will know that I am the LORD;
> those who wait for me shall not be put to shame. (49:23)

God's enemies will lick—eat—the dust, which means their future corresponds to the serpent's future.

The prophet Micah uses similar language about the shame of judgment:

The nations shall see and be ashamed of all their might;
they shall lay their hands on their mouths;
    their ears shall be deaf;
they shall lick the dust like a serpent,
    like the crawling things of the earth;
they shall come trembling out of their strongholds;
    they shall turn in dread to the LORD our God,
    and they shall be in fear of you. (7:16–17)

We see words about dust and a serpent, as well as licking—or eating—the dust.

The origin of this imagery in the Psalms and Prophets is the Torah, specifically Genesis 3:14–15. The enemies of God are under threat of judgment, just like their spiritual father. They are the seed of the serpent, the spiritual offspring of the evil one. Like the devil, they will eat the dust. The curse of God will be their everlasting future.

The Fountainhead

The defeat of the serpent in Genesis 3:14 is connected to a particular action in 3:15. And this latter verse is so important to the remainder of the Bible's storyline that we must not underestimate it. Here we arrive at the fountainhead of all messianic prophecy. This is the promise of a Son who will be born and defeat the serpent. It is this promise that the biblical authors advance and develop. It is this promise that the person and work of Christ fulfill.

The Lord said to the serpent, yet also in the hearing of the couple,

I will put enmity between you and the woman,
    and between your offspring and her offspring. (Gen. 3:15)

This half of the verse leads us to expect hostility, or tension, between the serpent's seed and the woman's seed. There is an interplay between individual and group references. The serpent is against the woman, and his seed is against her seed. But the offspring of the woman is not merely her descendants. An individual is in view, because in the second half of the verse, the Lord says, "He shall bruise your head, and you shall bruise his heel" (3:15).

He. His. These singular pronouns help us see that whatever hostility exists between the enemies of God and the people of God, the serpent's defeat is tied to the future birth of a Son. Because the serpent's judgment is good news, Genesis 3:15 is sometimes known as the *protoevangelium*, which means the "first gospel." According to Charles Simeon, "Now, as the oak with all its luxuriant branches is contained in the acorn, so was the whole of salvation, however copiously unfolded in subsequent revelations, comprehended in this one prophecy; which is, in fact, the sum and summary of the whole Bible."[1]

The redeeming hope for sinners flows from the fountainhead of Genesis 3:15. The Bible exists in order for sinners to know that God made this promise and how he kept it. As Jim Hamilton put it, the Old Testament is "a messianic document, written from a messianic perspective, to sustain a messianic hope."[2] The biblical authors intended to put forward in their writings a redemptive thread that develops, the way an acorn becomes an oak tree. Initially the promise is small and brief, but something epic and cosmic is contained in it. The storyline of Scripture narrates the unwavering faithfulness of God to that redemptive promise.

---

1 Charles Simeon, "The Seed of the Woman," discourse 7 in *Horae Homileticae*, vol. 1, *Genesis to Leviticus* (London: Holdsworth and Ball, 1832), 36.
2 James M. Hamilton Jr., "The Skull Crushing Seed of the Woman: Inner-Biblical Interpretation of Genesis 3:15," *Southern Baptist Journal of Theology* 10, no. 2 (2006): 31.

Let's reflect on what is exchanged between the future Son and the serpent: "he shall bruise your head, and you shall bruise his heel." The serpent receives a head wound, and the Son receives a heel wound. The description here is fitting because of the location of the serpent (on the ground) and the use of the Son's heel to strike (on the serpent's head). We're to imagine a person coming upon a serpent, the serpent striking the heel, and the heel coming down upon the serpent's head. At first glance, it may seem that only the serpent receives a death blow. Crushing a serpent's head, after all, means defeat. But should we picture a nonvenomous and ultimately harmless snake who bites the Son? Surely not. We should imagine a deadly serpent with a strike unto death.[3] The serpent strikes the Son, and the Son strikes the serpent.[4] The defeat of the serpent isn't without a price. The cost is the Son's life. Genesis 3:15 is a promise that the Son's victory will be accomplished through suffering and death.

A Hope in Motion

After the words of Genesis 3:15, readers are on the lookout for the promised seed, whose death will mean victory. But the storyline of

3   Kevin Chen argues this way: "Although it is common knowledge that such bites are not necessarily poisonous, the broader context of the Pentateuch suggests that the reader is supposed to understand the seed of the woman as suffering a poisonous snakebite, even a fatal one. This is because an important parallel passage in the Pentateuch references fatal snakebites. Numbers 21:4–6 describes Israel grumbling again and being bitten by 'fiery serpents' so that 'many people from Israel died.' This passage has additional words and themes in common with Genesis 3:15 that suggest an intentional intertextual relationship." *The Messianic Vision of the Pentateuch* (Downers Grove, IL: IVP Academic, 2019), 54. See also Deut. 32:24, 33, where poisonous snakebites are mentioned.

4   The two verbs translated "bruise" in Genesis 3:15 are identical in Hebrew. This may suggest that the same action is being administered—a strike unto death.

Scripture does not immediately announce his arrival. The Old Testament is a long and winding story of different covenants, empires, and centuries. The hope that is planted in Eden will grow, developing as the biblical authors give us insight into God's plan. Let's track examples of this hope as it is in motion.

In Genesis 5, there is a genealogy of Adam's descendants, and it stops in verse 32 with Noah. The writer gives us the reason for Noah's name: "When Lamech had lived 182 years, he fathered a son and called his name Noah, saying, 'Out of the ground that the LORD has cursed, this one shall bring us relief from our work and from the painful toil of our hands'" (5:28–29). One way to understand these two verses is that Lamech was hoping for the seed of the woman who would come, and he thought perhaps his son would be the one.

Now, of course, Noah wasn't the promised seed who would defeat the serpent. But the prophecy in Genesis 3:15 was a hope that Lamech—and thus others before him—knew about. Lamech's words also give more clarity on what the Son would accomplish. Lamech mentioned the cursed ground (which alludes to God's judgment in 3:17) and painful toil (which alludes to the conditions of work in 3:17–18). The coming Son "shall bring us relief" from these things. When we understand Genesis 3:15 and 5:29 together, we can discern that the coming Son would defeat the serpent and reverse the curse. This victory would mean relief for "us," Lamech said. The deliverer would act on behalf of sinners. His victory would mean their gain.

In Genesis 12, God sets apart the family of Abraham for the sake of all the families of the earth. God speaks about blessing five times in two verses (12:2–3). Before Genesis 12, we faced the problem of curse and judgment, and there was hope that a future Son would reverse the curse and overcome the ancient foe. Reversing a curse means you turn something from a curse into blessing. And in Genesis 12 we learn that God's plan to bless the families of the earth will be tied to a line of descent through Abraham's family.

Abraham was the father of a promised son in Genesis 22. Isaac would not reverse the curse, but his birth sustained the hope that a deliverer would come. When Abraham was willing to sacrifice Isaac at the Lord's instruction, the angel of Yahweh intervened at the last moment. Instead of Isaac being offered, a ram was offered (22:13). Abraham called the place "The LORD will provide" (22:14). God would provide the offering. The Genesis 3:15 Son would be the offering on behalf of sinners. God told Abraham, "And your offspring shall possess the gate of his enemies, and in your offspring shall all the nations of the earth be blessed, because you have obeyed my voice" (22:17–18). The offspring is viewed as the singular seed of Abraham who would defeat "his enemies." And this offspring's victory would also mean blessing for the nations of the world. The need for worldwide blessing is proportional to the worldwide problem of sin.

The future Son would be an Israelite from the tribe of Judah. A royal figure is in view when Jacob says to his son Judah,

> The scepter shall not depart from Judah,
> > nor the ruler's staff from between his feet,
> until tribute comes to him;
> > and to him shall be the obedience of the peoples. (Gen. 49:10)

This future Son from Judah's tribe will rule. He will be a new Adam, exercising dominion and being a blessing with his unending reign. Among the nations, he will receive honor and homage.

Outside Genesis, we can discern echoes of Genesis 3:15 in the prophecy of Balaam. The prophet Balaam was recruited to curse Israel, but all he could say in his pronouncements were good things for God's people. And in his final oracle, Balaam spoke of a future Israelite Son:

> I see him, but not now;
> I behold him, but not near:
> a star shall come out of Jacob,
> and a scepter shall rise out of Israel;
> it shall crush the forehead of Moab
> and break down all the sons of Sheth.
> Edom shall be dispossessed;
> Seir also, his enemies, shall be dispossessed.
> Israel is doing valiantly.
> And one from Jacob shall exercise dominion
> and destroy the survivors of cities! (Num. 24:17–19)

This prophecy in Numbers 24 is extraordinary because of the intertextual connections with earlier parts of the Torah. The scepter rising from Israel is reminiscent of the scepter and Judah's tribe from Genesis 49:10. The singular pronouns in Balaam's prophecy keep before us a promised Son from the family of Abraham, a Son who will rule. He shall overcome his enemies, just as Genesis 22:17–18 said. His victory even has a head-crushing image, reminding us of Genesis 3:15, where the coming Son would wound the serpent's head.

Beyond the Torah, we learn in 2 Samuel 7 that the promised seed—the royal Son from Judah's tribe—would descend from the house of David. The prophet Nathan told David the word of the Lord: "When your days are fulfilled and you lie down with your fathers, I will raise up your offspring after you, who shall come from your body, and I will establish his kingdom. He shall build a house for my name, and I will establish the throne of his kingdom forever" (2 Sam. 7:12–13). And in Micah 5:2 we learn that the Son of David's house would be born in David's hometown:

> But you, O Bethlehem Ephrathah,
>> who are too little to be among the clans of Judah,
> from you shall come forth for me
>> one who is to be ruler in Israel,
> whose coming forth is of old,
>> from ancient days.

The seed of the woman would be an Abrahamic descendant from Judah's tribe who would be a Davidic ruler born in the town of Bethlehem.

In the book of Isaiah, the reader sees prophecies of a servant of the Lord. The servant will come from Israel and will restore Israel (49:5–6). This figure will be

> a light for the nations,
>> that my [the Lord's] salvation may reach to the end of the
>>> earth. (49:6)

This concern of salvation reaching to the end of the earth recalls the blessing of Abraham that would go to the families of the earth through the promised Son. The Son of Abraham is the servant of the Lord in the book of Isaiah. This servant would face rejection, mistreatment, and suffering (50:6; 52:14; 53:3). In his suffering, he would bear the sorrows and griefs of sinners (53:4). He would be crushed for our iniquities (53:5). The substitutionary death of the suffering servant was the divine plan (53:10).

The death of Jesus on the cross was the fulfillment of Genesis 3:15. That ancient promise took an epic journey throughout the ages to the place where the Son of God laid down his life as the sin bearer and serpent crusher and curse reverser.

Enmity between Seeds

Across the span of history, there was enmity between the people of God and the enemies of God. These were installments—manifestations—of the larger spiritual enmity between the Lord and the evil one. The people of God are the seed of the woman, those whose spiritual allegiance is to their Creator and Redeemer. They believe his promises, receive his word, and hope in the deliverer. Unbelievers are the seed of the serpent, those whose spiritual allegiance is to their sin and against the Lord. They are captive to their iniquities, bound under the weight of their guilt.

One way to discern the unfolding narrative of Scripture is to see the larger enmity between the seed of the woman and the seed of the serpent. After the events of Genesis 3, Adam and Eve had two children named Cain and Abel. Though both sons brought offerings to God (4:3–4), the Lord did not receive Cain's offering, because of Cain's heart (4:5–7). Cain murdered his brother, though his brother was righteous and honored God. Spiritually speaking, we can conclude that Abel was part of the seed of the woman, the line of believers. Yet Cain demonstrated his spiritual condition too, that he was the seed of the serpent. John said that Cain "was of the evil one" (1 John 3:12).

Another manifestation of the hostility between the seed of the woman and the seed of the serpent is in Genesis 21, with Isaac and Ishmael. Isaac was the younger of the brothers, yet Ishmael had set himself against Isaac, mocking him and facing exile with his own mother (21:9–14). Though both boys had Abraham as their father, they didn't both have God as their spiritual Father. As Paul put it in Romans 9, "Not all are children of Abraham because they are his off-spring" (9:7). Being a child of Abraham—spiritually—meant that your heart hoped in God and that you had the faith of Abraham. Ishmael's actions revealed his heart, that he was the seed of the serpent.

The story of Israel's deliverance from Egyptian captivity is an expression of enmity between the seeds. Pharaoh and his oppressors were the seed of the serpent, and they were hostile toward the Israelites, the seed of the woman. When God brought out his people, the exodus led them to the Red Sea, and between the walls of water they walked on dry ground. The day of their salvation, however, meant judgment for the Egyptians. The Egyptian army pursued the Israelites, but God brought the walls of water upon them and crushed his enemies. He defeated the seed of the serpent. He accomplished salvation through judgment, all for the glory of his name.[5]

In the book of Judges, a wicked general named Sisera fled and sought refuge in the tent of a woman named Jael (4:7, 17). Jael invited him in and gave him drink and warmth. But things were not what they seemed. He asked her to stand watch at the tent opening so that they could send away anyone searching for him. When he fell asleep, Jael "took a tent peg, and took a hammer in her hand. Then she went

---

5   For a book-length argument that the center of biblical theology is the glory of God in salvation through judgment, see James M. Hamilton Jr, *God's Glory in Salvation through Judgment: A Biblical Theology* (Wheaton, IL: Crossway, 2010).

softly to him and drove the peg into his temple until it went down into the ground while he was lying fast asleep from weariness. So he died" (4:21). The seed of the serpent—Sisera—was overcome by a fatal head wound.

Before David was king of the land of Israel, he defeated a gigantic Philistine named Goliath, and David's victory reminds us of Genesis 3:15. Goliath was a mighty warrior who represented the Philistines, the seed of the serpent. Even the description of Goliath is serpent-like. He "had a helmet of bronze on his head, and he was armed with a coat of mail, and the weight of the coat was five thousand shekels of bronze. And he had bronze armor on his legs, and a javelin of bronze slung between his shoulders" (1 Sam. 17:5–6). The armor was like scales over his body. Young David took some stones, put one in a sling, and defeated the warrior. The serpent-warrior was overcome by a head wound: "And David put his hand in his bag and took out a stone and slung it and struck the Philistine on his forehead. The stone sank into his forehead, and he fell on his face to the ground" (17:49). This head wound was then followed by a head removal. "David ran and stood over the Philistine and took his sword and drew it out of its sheath and killed him and cut off his head with it" (17:51). David, the seed of the woman, was victorious.

Many more Old Testament examples of the enmity between the seed of the serpent and the seed of the woman could be offered. The shadows of Genesis 3:15 are seen all over the storyline of Scripture. When we see God's enemies rise against his people, we anticipate his delivering hand. And when his people seem to succumb to the wiles and snares of the wicked, we trust that the temporal victories of the wicked will be undone by the King who is just.

According to the New Testament Gospels, Jesus was opposed throughout his earthly ministry. Here was the true seed of the woman, the one who would do battle against the serpent, and along the way the serpent's seed gathered against him. Religious leaders laid out tests and snares, acting like the evil one who tempted him in the wilderness (Matt. 21:23; 22:15, 23, 34–35; cf. 4:1–11). Jesus's words to the religious leaders exposed their spiritual condition:

> If God were your Father, you would love me, for I came from God and I am here. I came not of my own accord, but he sent me. Why do you not understand what I say? It is because you cannot bear to hear my word. You are of your father the devil, and your will is to do your father's desires. (John 8:42–44)

The religious leaders who opposed Jesus revealed that they were the seed of the serpent, even though they were ethnic Israelites. If you aligned yourself against Jesus, you were aligning yourself with that ancient serpent the devil—the dragon.

The Dragon's Present and Future

Genesis 3:15 prophesied victory over the serpent, and the cross inaugurated this victory. The return of Christ will bring final and everlasting judgment against the evil one. The present-day activities of Satan can be seen in Revelation 12. The promised Son has defeated him, and yet he makes war against the seed of the woman, who are those united to the Son through faith.

John wrote that "the dragon became furious with the woman and went off to make war on the rest of her offspring, on those who keep the commandments of God and hold to the testimony of Jesus"

(Rev. 12:17). The warfare of the dragon is depicted in 1 Peter 5:8: "Your adversary the devil prowls around like a roaring lion, seeking someone to devour." Though the devil has been defeated and his judgment is sure, he remains the adversary of God's people. He is the constant accuser and the arch blasphemer. He seeks to devour. That is his relentless mission.

The present raging of the dragon can be seen in the book of Acts when the apostles and disciples face hostility from Jews and Gentiles, from synagogue parishioners and political leaders. By assembling against God's people, the seed of the serpent is assembling against the Lord Jesus. When the seed of the serpent opposes the Lord and the Lord's people, the will of the dragon is being done.

Yet the dragon will fail, and his judgment day will come. Revelation 20 says, "The devil who had deceived them was thrown into the lake of fire and sulfur where the beast and the false prophet were, and they will be tormented day and night forever and ever" (20:10). The prophecy about the serpent in Genesis 3:15 is pointing to Revelation 20:10. On that day, when righteous judgment is applied far and wide and to all, the evil one will enter his everlasting sentence. As Isaiah put it, "In that day the Lord with his hard and great and strong sword will punish Leviathan the fleeing serpent, Leviathan the twisting serpent, and he will slay the dragon that is in the sea" (Isa. 27:1).

The church of Christ faces tumult and suffering, sorrows and temptations. The evil one prowls and rages. But this is not the church's future. The church is triumphant in Christ. We are more than conquerors through Christ who loved us and loves us (Rom. 8:37). Believers may face betrayal and rejection and suffering, even martyrdom, yet Jesus promised his followers: "Not a hair of your head will perish. By your endurance you will gain your lives" (Luke 21:18–19). Death is gain for the Christian, because death brings us into the presence of the Christ we love.

Satan may be raging now, but his future position is beneath our feet. Paul told the Romans: "The God of peace will soon crush Satan under your feet. The grace of our Lord Jesus Christ be with you" (Rom. 16:20). These hope-giving words allude to Genesis 3:15, which promises that the seed of the woman will defeat Satan. Who is the seed? Certainly Christ, but also those who are in Christ. Christ destroyed "the one who has the power of death, that is, the devil" (Heb. 2:14). The promised Son crushed the serpent, and because we are united to the Son, we will crush him too.

This Christian Life

The impact of Genesis 3:15 on subsequent Scripture is profound and far-reaching. Bible readers will feel the reverberations of Genesis 3:15 all the way to the end of Revelation. Especially crucial for our faith is the recognition that the river of messianic prophecy flows from that verse. As we track the storyline of Scripture, we see that the divine plan is the death of the promised Son. The Lord Jesus accomplishes salvation through judgment.

We are united to the serpent crusher. The royal Son, who came to bring blessing to the families of the earth, loves us and will return for us. Our lives may not seem victorious now, but we don't see all that is, and we certainly don't see all that will be. Satan may be a roaring lion seeking to devour, but Jesus is the Lion of Judah seeking to deliver.

The words of judgment upon the serpent in Genesis 3:14–15 are words of salvation for sinners. The curse-reversing grace of God would take on flesh. The last Adam would come to bring a redemptive kingdom where life and new creation overcome corruption and death. We need the whole storyline of Scripture to see the fullness of divine wisdom in redeeming sinners. The first prophecy sets the stage and trajectory: a future Son would be born who would crush the serpent through death—salvation through judgment. And during the first-century Roman Empire, outside the city of Jerusalem a cross was raised up. The seed of the woman appeared defeated by the serpent's lethal strike. But ancient words were being fulfilled. On Good Friday, a holy heel took aim with all the power of heaven.

9

Multiplication and Division

ON THE DAY MY OLDEST SON WAS BORN, I was privy to the wonder of childbirth. But before the baby's arrival, my wife experienced predictable discomfort and pain. Caught up in the excitement of what was happening, I told her, "This is what Genesis 3 was talking about!" Then I paraphrased verse 16 in the hospital room. That was the wrong time for the right verse. If my wife is a reliable sample of birthing mothers, then no one in labor has ever felt better by hearing Genesis 3:16: "I will surely multiply your pain in childbearing."

Every birth has occurred outside Eden, and childbirth is associated with discomfort and pain. Why does such a blessing come with these challenges? What about the relational difficulties that a mother and wife can face? One of the purposes of Genesis 3 is to provide insight into why the troubles of the world are what they are. We all wake up every day outside Eden, and the trials and temptations of this life cause pressure on every level—personally, relationally, societally. Wherever sinners dwell, tensions will arise to some degree at some point. The pains and griefs of life are loud cries of a broken creation longing for redemption, for new creation.

Pain in Childbearing

The difficulties of life in a fallen world wouldn't take Adam and Eve completely by surprise. Before they left the garden of Eden, the Lord told them some things to expect. After addressing the serpent (Gen. 3:14–15), God spoke to the woman (3:16) and then the man (3:17–19). In the present chapter, we will reflect on the divine words to the woman. Confronted while hiding among trees, the woman and man learned that sin had consequences. In 3:16 the Lord God told her:

> I will surely multiply your pain in childbearing;
> > in pain you shall bring forth children.
> Your desire shall be contrary to your husband,
> > but he shall rule over you.

The first two lines are parallel: God promised to multiply pain in childbearing, and then he announced that in pain the woman would bring forth children. These two claims speak in a cause-effect relationship: God would multiply pain, and as a result of this pain, she would bring forth children.

This judgment is connected to the commission in Genesis 1:28: "Be fruitful and multiply and fill the earth and subdue it, and have dominion over the fish of the sea and over the birds of the heavens and over every living thing that moves on the earth." The call to be fruitful and multiply wasn't revoked in Genesis 3, but now a judgment would factor in its fulfillment. Multiplying descendants would come through multiplied pain. Children would be a blessing, but their arrival would signal the brokenness of this present age.

The forces of death would be at work in the fallen world. While Eve had not physically died, despite eating from the forbidden tree (Gen. 3:6–7), the fulfillment of God's warning (2:17) came in stages. Pain and suffering were shadows of death's presence. And now pain would be associated with life emerging into this world.

The word "childbearing" can also be translated "pregnancy" or "conception." This promise in Genesis 3:16, therefore, could involve more than the difficulties in childbirth. The womb can face the sorrows of barrenness and miscarriages. Long before the pain of childbirth itself, there may be pains associated with becoming pregnant and carrying children to term. These challenges do not mean that the individual woman is facing God's judgment, but she is seeking to carry out the Genesis 1:28 commission in a broken world.

Narratives elsewhere in Genesis tell of barren women. Abraham married Sarah, who was barren; Isaac married Rebekah, who was barren; Jacob married Rachel, who was barren. These mothers experienced the distress and sadness of an empty womb. They were women seeking to multiply with their husbands in a fallen world, yet their desires were mixed with the grief of prolonged childlessness. At one point Rachel told Jacob, "Give me children, or I shall die!" (Gen. 30:1). He replied, "Am I in the place of God, who has withheld from you the fruit of the womb?" (30:2).

Children would be a blessing and a fulfillment of the commission in Genesis 1:28, but progeny would come through pain.

First Cain, Then Abel

The first births are reported in Genesis 4. When the woman "conceived and bore Cain" (4:1), she experienced what God had promised in Genesis 3:16. Then "she bore his brother Abel" (4:2). These events fulfilled Genesis 1:28 and 3:16 at the same time. No longer were there only two image bearers. Adam and Eve had two sons.

Cain was the first son of Eve. Since God had promised that a seed of the woman would come to defeat the serpent, we can understand her words at Cain's birth—"I have gotten a man with the help of the LORD" (Gen. 4:1)—as hoping that God was fulfilling the promise he had made. But Cain's murder of his brother showed that Cain wasn't the seed who would defeat the serpent. Cain was like the serpent.

Pain in childbearing gave way to pain in childrearing. A mom and dad became sinners parenting sinners. The psalmist Solomon was right to say,

> Behold, children are a heritage from the LORD,
>> the fruit of the womb a reward. (Ps. 127:3)

Yet Solomon also said,

> A wise son makes a glad father,
>> but a foolish son is a sorrow to his mother. (Prov. 10:1)

Adam and Eve knew what it was like to have a wise son and a foolish son. Eve knew the sorrow of a grieving mother. She knew the pain of bearing a child and then seeing that child grow in wickedness rather than the fear of the Lord. Adam knew a father's gladness when he thought of Abel, yet that gladness turned to grief when Cain destroyed this heritage of godliness.

The pain of childbearing brought forth another child: "Adam knew his wife again, and she bore a son and called his name Seth, for she said, 'God has appointed for me another offspring instead of Abel, for Cain killed him'" (Gen. 4:25). This statement from Eve is probably her renewed hope in a victorious seed, since at that point her only other son was like the serpent. Perhaps she thought that Seth would be the one who would crush the serpent's head. With the death of Abel, the serpent seemed to triumph. The birth of Seth was the light of hope that God would keep his promise of deliverance for sinners. Genesis 5 traces the line of Seth. And we also learn that Adam and Eve "had other sons and daughters" after Seth was born (5:4). These many births lead us to affirm that image bearers were multiplying in a world where pain in childbearing reminded them that all was not well.

A Sword in the Soul

In the days of Caesar Augustus, a virgin named Mary gave birth to a son named Jesus, just as the angel Gabriel had said (Luke 1:26–38; 2:1–7). When the time for that birth had come, she and Joseph were in Bethlehem, and "she gave birth to her firstborn son and wrapped him in swaddling cloths and laid him in a manger" (2:7).

At last the seed of the woman had come. The distant son of Eve was the son of Mary, and Mary's son had come to crush the serpent's head. But Mary's childbearing experience was like the ones she knew already from the mouths of other mothers. There was the passing of months until the time arrived for birth. She had the usual cramps and discomfort, sickness and aches. Mary, who knew the Torah and thus knew Genesis 3:16, brought forth in pain the one who would reverse the curse and bear our pain.

The pain Mary experienced in birthing our Lord would be surpassed by her agony and distress at what would happen to him during the climax of his earthly ministry. She learned that heartache was in store for her because a man named Simeon prophesied about the future state of her soul. When she and Joseph brought baby Jesus to the temple, Simeon told her, "Behold, this child is appointed for the fall and rising of many in Israel, and for a sign that is opposed (and a sword will pierce through your own soul also), so that thoughts from many hearts may be revealed" (Luke 2:34–35).

Jesus's ministry revealed the spiritual condition of people's hearts. The Israelites were divided over him, especially the religious leaders. The appointed Son faced fierce opposition. Depending on how people responded to Jesus, some would be lifted up and others brought low. How could these things be easy for a mother to watch?

At Jesus's crucifixion, he saw his mother nearby, who was watching the gruesome event unfold. Another disciple (probably John) was standing nearby. Jesus said to his mother, "Woman, behold, your son!" And to the disciple he said, "Behold, your mother!" (John 19:26–27). Surely on that day of Jesus's crucifixion, the sword that Simeon mentioned pierced Mary's soul. She had known pain, but not like this. Her son, her Lord, was affixed to the judgment tree.

Speaking of Pain

The opening line of Genesis 3:16 contains the first use of the word "pain" in the Bible. With the consequences of sin, suffering comes into the world. This same word is used in God's words to Adam in Genesis 3:17 and in Lamech's explanation of naming his son Noah in Genesis 5:29. Pain is now part of our human experience, but the coming deliverer would do something about our pain.

The prophet Isaiah told of the future Messiah, who would be our faithful substitute, and in our place he would bear our sorrows. Isaiah called him "a man of sorrows" (Isa. 53:3), or "a man of *pains*." Isaiah said that this humble and suffering servant "has borne our griefs and carried our sorrows" (53:4), "our *pains*." He's called a man of pains because of what he carried for us. In a world where sinners reap what they sow, Jesus came to reap what he did not sow. He came to bear our transgressions and pain. When Jesus was bearing pain on the cross, he was cutting out sin at the root. By bearing our sorrows and pains, he was defeating the curse from the inside.

God moves toward the sufferer. He is not indifferent to pain. In Exodus 3, Moses encounters the Lord at the burning bush, and the Lord explains why he is going to deliver the Israelites out of Egypt: "I have surely seen the affliction of my people who are in Egypt and have heard their cry because of their taskmasters. I know their sufferings" (Ex. 3:7). That last word is God's claim to know their *pains*. Unable to escape from their pains, sinners behold the rescuing grace of God.

The good news of the gospel is that God's rescuing grace has taken on flesh, and we call him Jesus. On the cross, he experienced pain so that he might bear our pains. His mother Mary bore him in pain so that he might reverse the effects of the fall. The plan of God would unfold in a world where affliction touches every human life, including the manner in which life comes into the fallen world.

While Genesis 3:16 is the first mention of pain in the Bible, Revelation 21:4 is the last mention. In John's apocalyptic vision of the future, he saw a new heaven and new earth, for the former heaven and earth had passed away (Rev. 21:1). The dwelling place of God will be with us, and we will be his people forever (21:3). John says the Lord "will wipe away every tear from their eyes, and death shall be no more, neither shall there be mourning, nor crying, nor pain anymore, for the former things have passed away" (21:4).

Pain belongs to the "former things," and we're living in the remainder of these former things now. But, as God's people, we do not anticipate the frequent or seldom experience of pain. Pain will be no more. The fullness of Christ's finished work on the cross will mean relief from the effects of the fall. We will be raised from the dead, glorified. Pain is our experience only in this life. Christ will come to make all things new. Until then, the creation moans and joins the laments of sorrow and pain in this world. Paul wrote, "For we know that the whole creation has been groaning together in the pains of childbirth until now" (Rom. 8:22). *The pains of childbirth*. What an apt metaphor. These pains are cries for liberation, for the freedom of glory and restoration. Lift up your heads, all you saints. Though pain is multiplied now, the coming glory will surpass it all.

The Second Half

There are two parts to Genesis 3:16. If the first half is about multiplication, the second half is about division.

> Your desire shall be contrary to your husband,
>> but he shall rule over you.

The effects of sin will be evident in the woman's experiences as a mother and as a wife. This part of the verse doesn't mean, of course, that unmarried women or women without children will evade the effects of sin. But since Eve was already a wife and would soon be a mother, she would experience the effects of sin in those relationships.

Since God's words to the serpent were all negative for the serpent (Gen. 3:14–15), and since God's words to the man were all negative for the man (3:17–19), it is reasonable to assume that God's words to the woman were also negative (3:16). But not all interpreters see this desire as negative. The translation can be simply "Your desire shall be for your husband," or even, "Your desire shall be toward your husband." That doesn't have to be a wrongful desire. What if God promised pain in childbearing but then assured the woman that she would still have sexual desire for her husband? This statement could then function as assurance to the woman. The pain of childbearing would not mean that sexual intimacy with her husband was a problem. If the woman's "desire" is positive here, how does that square with the last line, that her husband "shall rule over" her? The last line could mean that while the woman will rightly desire her husband, he may be tempted to dominate her.

Interpreters could also understand the woman's desire as negative and the husband's ruling as negative as well. The strength of this reading increases when it is examined alongside Genesis 4:7, which is just fifteen verses later in the narrative. There is similar wording and syntax construction, and the close proximity of these verses may suggest a negative understanding of the woman's desire. In Genesis 4, the Lord tells Cain: "If you do well, will you not be accepted? And if you do not do well, sin is crouching at the door. Its desire is contrary to you, but you must rule over it" (4:7). Look at the relevant constructions in 3:16 and 4:7.

| Genesis 3:16 | "Your desire shall be contrary to your husband," | "but he shall rule over you." |
| Genesis 4:7 | "Its desire is contrary to you," | "but you must rule over it." |

In Genesis 4:7, sin's desire is seeking something bad. Sin is "crouching at the door" and desiring to dominate Cain. But Cain hears that he must rule over it. Dominate or be dominated; kill or be killed. If we can legitimately read the constructions in 3:16 and 4:7 as mutually interpretive, then God was telling the woman about a desire for domination that she should resist. And the man would be dominating too, either initially or in response to the woman.

Certainty seems elusive. We should approach the latter part of Genesis 3:16 with interpretive humility, recognizing the difficulties that interpreters have noticed. The word "desire" cannot be determinative by itself, since the Hebrew noun only occurs three times in the Old Testament (Gen. 3:16; 4:7; Song 7:10). Its meaning in the Song of Songs isn't negative: "I am my beloved's, and his desire is for me."[1] The context in Genesis 3 and other literary considerations (like the proximity of 4:7) must guide us.

The similarities between Genesis 3:16 and 4:7 suggest that the woman's desire for her husband is a wrongful one. Instead of "desire shall be for" or "desire shall be toward," the ESV translates the phrase "desire shall be contrary to" in order to make the negative connotation of her desire clear. This is not a sexual desire for her husband. The negative framing of this desire is supported by the last line of 3:16 ("but he shall rule over you") as well as by the wholly negative content for those addressed by the Lord in 3:14–15 (the serpent) and 3:17–19 (the man). The woman's "desire" and the

---

1   Since Song 7:10 uses a word for "desire" that is otherwise found only in Gen. 3:16 and 4:7, we can reasonably infer that an allusion to Genesis is deliberate. Notice the direction of desire in the Genesis and Song of Solomon contexts. In Gen. 3:16 the woman's desire is for the man, while in Song 7:10 the man's desire is for the woman. The larger context in Gen. 3 is one of judgment and consequence. The larger context in Song 7 is delight and invitation. What if Song 7:10 is picturing a reversal of the effects of the fall that Gen. 3:16 articulated? If Song 7:10 is saying something positive, by way of reversing an earlier condition, then this textual connection could support a negative view of "desire" in Gen. 3:16.

man's "rule" in Genesis 3:16 should probably be understood as negative attitudes (which manifest in actions) in the husband and wife toward each other.

While we shouldn't interpret Genesis 3:16 to mean that every wife seeks to dominate her husband or that every husband seeks to dominate his wife, we can recognize that mistreatment and manipulation in marriage are temptations that spouses face. Sometimes one spouse is passive while the other seeks to rule. In other marriages both spouses vie for control, trying to subdue the personality and preferences of one another.

Seeking Self First

In order for a wife to dominate her husband or for a husband to dominate his wife, each must put self first, self above all. The husband thinks of what he wants and how to get it and what is in his way. Perhaps what is in his way is his wife's preferences or plans. The wife, in like fashion, may seek her own interests above all, contravening her husband and seeing him as a means to her own ends.

Consider the marital disasters that ensue when a spouse places self above all. When self is put first, all manner of sins become justifiable: selfishness, deceit, manipulation, anger, impatience, immorality, and more. An abiding danger in marriage outside Eden is that you will seek to exercise dominion over the person you're called to love, encourage, support, value, cherish, and enjoy.

The notion of dominion is important, because the second half of Genesis 3:16 connects to the commission in 1:28, just as the first half of 3:16 did. God had told the couple, "Be fruitful and multiply and fill the earth and subdue it, and have dominion over the fish of the sea and over the birds of the heavens and over every living thing that moves on the earth" (1:28). The woman learned in 3:16 that this multiplying of descendants would be a blessing touched by pain. And the responsibility to subdue creation would also tempt the couple to subdue one another. They were told to be fruitful together and to subdue the earth together. But never was one of them told to subdue, or exercise dominion over, the other. Let's group the language in 3:16 with 1:28:

| Genesis 1:28 | "Be fruitful and multiply and fill the earth" | "and subdue it, and have dominion . . ." |
| Genesis 3:16 | "I will surely multiply your pain in childbearing; / in pain you shall bring forth children." | "Your desire shall be contrary to your husband, / but he shall rule over you." |

A domineering wife or husband dishonors God. Creation should be subdued by men and women because men and women are image bearers. And they are image bearers equally. As male and female, each is endowed with dignity and worth. The woman is not greater than the man, nor is the man more worthy than the woman. The covenant of marriage is the union of two image bearers called to love and be faithful to one another.

This language in Genesis 3:16 does not nullify God's design for the husband to lead, cherish, and protect his wife (Eph. 5:25–30, 33), but it does recognize that in a fallen world, a husband will be tempted to forsake his responsibilities and to put himself first, either by passively resigning or by aggressively dominating. This language in Genesis 3:16 does not nullify God's design for the wife to respect and submit to her husband's leadership (Eph. 5:22–24, 33), but it does recognize that in a fallen world, a wife will be tempted to dominate or control her husband, either by passively undermining him or by actively subduing him.

A marriage covenant ought not to be a battle for dominion. When one spouse is seeking to control or subdue the other, the ground becomes ripe for verbal, emotional, and physical abuse to grow. This toxic fruit diminishes the covenant of marriage and creates resentment and suspicion in the relationship. The lines in Genesis 3:16 confirm that turning from God's wisdom is disastrous. Doing what is right in our own eyes doesn't lead to human flourishing. Forsaking God's commands is a surefire way to live poorly with others by promoting self above all, pointing fingers in blame, and hiding your own shame from others and especially from God.

Discord and strife are not unusual in marriage. The reality of being married outside Eden is that you are a sinner in covenant with a sinner, and you both need to walk with humility and openness before one another and the living God who joined you together. There was once a time when "the man and his wife were both naked and were not ashamed" (Gen. 2:25). Despite conflict in marriage, the goal and overarching desire ought to be movement toward relational honesty, embrace, trust building, and treating one another with dignity and respect.

When we put self first, we will not love our neighbor well. We will disrespect, demean, and use others, including our spouse. This is not of Christ. Remember that the serpent was the one who twisted and exploited, who came with an agenda to impose on another, and who sought to subdue. It goes without saying, but let's say it anyway: the serpent's ways are no model for marriage.

This Christian Life

In the story God is telling through his word, we learn that pain and conflict are part of life inside and outside our homes. God is leading his people into everlasting joy together with him, but this road "under the sun" goes through valleys of despair and over mountains of strife. Each day we are being invited again to trust God's plan to make all things new and to work all things for the good of his people.

Trust is difficult because we know about pain. Maybe you have experienced the frustration of trying to get pregnant or the devastation of a miscarriage. Maybe you know the pain of childbirth and childrearing. Maybe you have endured the conflicts that come in a marriage covenant. Maybe you know the disappointments that come with unmet expectations. Maybe you have felt the cold shoulder, heard the blaming voice, or hidden sin in shame. Have you felt the impulse to control your spouse and dominate with your words? Have you behaved as if you were more important than your spouse and as if he or she can be safely ignored or denied? Have you noticed how blessings like having children and being married can also be mixed with sorrow?

We need to let the words of Genesis 3:16 speak to the situations of our lives. After all, that verse comes in a chapter explaining why things are the way they are. But the reason we can be hopeful is that the way things are isn't the way they will always be. One day these things will be the "former things," passed away under the new creation power of the King.

This world, and everyone in it, is perishing. The pain in us and around us is a deafening announcement that not all is right.

But God has loved this broken world, and he sent his Son into it through the pains of childbirth, that he might be broken and bear our brokenness, becoming the man of pains for us. All who believe in him will not ultimately perish. Their future is life to the full because their future is Christ. The answer to Genesis 3:16 is John 3:16.

10

From Dust to Dust

DO YOU EVER LOOK AROUND at your life and see futility? So much is the same. Routines and habits abound. Do you ever wonder what gain there is in what you do? And does it ever dawn on you that no matter how much you work, you are heading toward the dust? There is no avoiding death, no matter your gym regimen or daily diet or vitamin supplements.

Growing up, we come to discover the hardness of life. There is real pain, real toil, real evil. The more we go through and the more we see others endure, we may ask if there is any relief to come. Adam and the generations after him would live in a fallen world, a creation marred by sin and corruption. Life outside Eden would not be like life inside Eden. Adam would know the difference by experience. He would have memories of the garden he'd inhabited. But before he left, he learned what to expect for the rest of his days. As we reflect on what he learned, we will be better equipped to glorify God in this brief earthly life.

A Rival Voice

Having spoken to the serpent (Gen. 3:14–15) and to the woman (3:16), God then spoke to the man. He told Adam (3:17–19):

Because you have listened to the voice of your wife
>   and have eaten of the tree
of which I commanded you,
>   "You shall not eat of it,"
cursed is the ground because of you;
>   in pain you shall eat of it all the days of your life;
thorns and thistles it shall bring forth for you;
>   and you shall eat the plants of the field.
By the sweat of your face
>   you shall eat bread,
till you return to the ground,
>   for out of it you were taken;
for you are dust,
>   and to dust you shall return.

God pronounced that the ground was cursed, but this pronouncement came after a lead-up about what Adam did. The situation is summarized as eating from the prohibited tree. The first recorded words of God to Adam were about the garden's trees: "You may surely eat of every tree of the garden, but of the tree of the knowledge of good and evil you shall not eat, for in the day that you eat of it you shall surely die" (Gen. 2:16–17). And in 3:17, God recounts what the man has done: "eaten of the tree of which I commanded you, 'You shall not eat of it.'" Adam had known the commandment, as well as the punishment, yet he ate anyway.

Adam was not the first to eat. He ate after his wife. God's words in Genesis 3:17 open with "Because you have listened to the voice of your wife and have eaten." Adam chose her words over God's words. God's words and his wife's words did not say the same thing about the tree. When we look back in Genesis 3:6 to the moment the man ate the fruit, there is no mention of his wife's voice. We should probably understand that the eating scene contained words we are not told.

What might the voice of his wife have said? "Nothing happened once I bit this. Do you want some?" Or if he thought about intervening, did she say, "The serpent assured me that everything would be fine." Maybe she showed him the fruit and didn't want to eat alone. "You're not going to just stand there, are you? Take a bite. We're in this together." Or maybe the voice of his wife simply echoed the voice of the serpent: "We will not surely die, Adam. For God knows that when we eat of it, our eyes will be opened, and we will be like God, knowing good and evil" (see Gen. 3:4–5). Whatever she said, Adam listened. Since he had already heard about the prohibited tree (Gen. 2:16–17), his action in Genesis 3:6 showed that he believed his wife and not the Lord.

Sometimes in the Old Testament, a character is depicted as wrongly listening to a rival voice. Rather than doing what would honor the Lord and demonstrate trust in the Lord, a character will heed a voice that directs otherwise. In Genesis 16, for example, Abram has already learned that God will grant him a son. But when time passes and Sarai has not yet borne him a child, she tells him: "Behold now, the LORD has prevented me from bearing children. Go in to my servant; it may be that I shall obtain children by her" (16:2). The servant was Hagar. And Abraham "listened to the voice of Sarai" (16:2).

A different situation arises in Job's story. The man Job has faced tremendous loss and physical affliction (Job 1:13–22; 2:1–8). His wife tells him: "Do you still hold fast your integrity? Curse God and die" (2:9). She responds very differently than her husband to the tragedy. Job has earlier fallen on the ground, worshiped the Lord, and declared that the

Lord's name should be blessed (1:21). The voice of his wife, on the other hand, calls on Job to curse the Lord, which Job refuses to do. He tells her, "You speak as one of the foolish women would speak" (2:10). In this story, Job refuses to listen to the voice that would turn him from God.

Rival voices will always be around us, pointing us away from God and sowing seeds of distrust in our hearts. We will be blessed if we do not listen to them. Blessed is the person who does not follow wicked counsel, stand in the path of sinners, or sit where the scoffers' seats are marked (Ps. 1:1).

Cursed Ground

Having listened to the voice of his wife, Adam ate from the tree of the knowledge of good and evil. Therefore, God said, "Cursed is the ground because of you." The nature of this curse is clearer in the phrases that come next, but let's realize that for the second time in Genesis 3, God pronounced the word "cursed." The first time was to the serpent: "Cursed are you above all livestock" (3:14). And now we hear the words to the man: "Cursed is the ground because of you" (3:17).

Though the woman ate first, Adam's federal headship is on display in Genesis 3:17. The ground was cursed because of him, not because of her. How much of the ground outside Eden is affected by God's pronouncement? All of it. Departing from Eden would mean stepping onto ground that exists under divine curse. God's words bring this judgment to pass because his words are effective and powerful. When God said, "Let there be light," there was light (1:3). When God said, "Cursed is the ground," the result would be according to his word.

Adam's relationship with the ground was personal. We read in Genesis 2:7 that the Lord "formed the man of dust from the ground and breathed into his nostrils the breath of life, and the man became a living creature." The ground would now resist Adam's work and investment. He would "eat the plants of the field" and "eat bread" (3:18–19). But working the ground would be toilsome.

The difficulty of work wasn't a short-term situation. God told Adam, "In pain you shall eat of it [the ground] all the days of your life" (Gen. 3:17) and "till you return to the ground, for out of it you were taken" (3:19). The blessing wrapped in this promise is that Adam would eat. Food would come. But Adam's work would be in "pain," and this is the same word God used when he addressed the woman in Genesis 3:16 ("I will surely multiply your pain in childbearing").

In Genesis 2:15, God puts Adam in the garden of Eden "to work it and keep it." Soon to leave Eden, Adam would have the responsibility to work the ground, yet this work would be done in pain and "by the sweat of your face" (3:19). There would be a kind of a hostility between the man and the earth. According to Paul, creation is in "bondage to corruption" (Rom. 8:21). The ground, like us, is short of glory. But its freedom is coming. Paul wrote that creation "will be set free" and "obtain the freedom of the glory of the children of God" (8:21).

We see, in the meantime, floods and fires. There are storms and tsunamis. Volcanoes erupt, and avalanches wreak havoc. The sun, which provides light and sight, is the same sun with rays that can cause severe burns and even cancer. Cold temperatures can harm your body and, in freezing conditions, can kill you. Every disaster is an audible groan for freedom. Every cry and every health catastrophe is a desperate plea for deliverance from this bondage to corruption.

Thorns and Thistles

Until that day of glorious liberation, the ground shall bring forth "thorns and thistles" (Gen. 3:18). That is not a throwaway detail.

Thorns and thistles hurt. They symbolize pain. They make you think twice before touching. The promise of thorns and thistles must imply that these things were not present in Eden. Unfamiliar with thorns and thistles, Adam would soon discover what they were.

The ground wouldn't yield only thorns and thistles, however. Food would grow, such as plants of the field (Gen. 3:18). In this way God would provide for his image bearers. Yet the presence of thorns would be an abiding reminder of these garden consequences, a sign of what happened when the head of humanity exchanged the truth of God for a lie. The ground was cursed.

Thorns also symbolized that the ground would have trouble, that it could be difficult to cultivate, and even that much sweat and toil might accomplish very little. The notion of trouble with land is seen in various prophetic texts. In Isaiah 32:13, the prophet mentions

> the soil of my people
> > growing up in thorns and briers.

In Isaiah 33:9 he says,

> The land mourns and languishes;
> > Lebanon is confounded and withers away;
> Sharon is like a desert,
> > and Bashan and Carmel shake off their leaves.

The prophet sounds a word of judgment in Isaiah 34:13:

> Thorns shall grow over its strongholds,
> > nettles and thistles in its fortresses.

It shall be the haunt of jackals,
    an abode for ostriches.

The imagery of thorns conveys an unhabitable place—or, at the very least, a place that needs to be subdued and cultivated. Widespread thorns and thistles do not evoke a picture of flourishing and blessing. When God wants to stir hope for renewal and new creation, he often describes changes in the land, on the ground. We know from Genesis 3:17–19 that the ground is cursed, but God's plan is to overcome this curse with blessing.

In Isaiah 35:1–2, the Lord says:

The wilderness and the dry land shall be glad;
    the desert shall rejoice and blossom like the crocus;
it shall blossom abundantly
    and rejoice with joy and singing.
The glory of Lebanon shall be given to it,
    the majesty of Carmel and Sharon.
They shall see the glory of the LORD,
    the majesty of our God.

God's blessing upon the land is a reminder that creation's bondage to corruption will not last. There are glimpses of glory here and now. We see the transition from winter to spring. We see leaves grow again on trees, crops rise from the ground, fruit become visible on the vines. We see the butterfly emerge from the chrysalis. Flowers blossom as life conquers death, as beauty triumphs over decay.

Thorns and thistles are signs of the present state of things, but these present things will one day be the former things.

To the Dust

The futility of life under the sun is suggested by the inevitability of death. God told Adam—and, through him, all of us—that despite the sweat and labor required for life in this world, Adam would "return to the ground, for out of it you were taken" (Gen. 3:19). Adam's earthly origin was his earthly destiny: "for you are dust, and to dust you shall return" (3:19).

The dust claims the wise and the fool, the rich and the poor, the strong and the weak. No one escapes the dust. You can't work hard enough or be clever enough or wait long enough to evade the inevitable. The writer of Ecclesiastes gives us profound meditations on this fleeting life. He asks,

> What does man gain by all the toil
>   at which he toils under the sun? (1:3)

You could respond with, "Money, clothing, shelter," but material things aren't on the writer's mind. It's obvious that there is short-term gain for toil. But what about long-term? The writer has death on his mind: "A generation goes, and a generation comes," he says in the next verse (1:4).

Much of Ecclesiastes is a reflection on our Genesis 3 world. Life is fleeting, and toil seems futile. Anything we gain in an earthly sense will soon be lost to us and passed on to another. "I hated all my toil in which I toil under the sun, seeing that I must leave it to the man who will come after me, and who knows whether he will be wise or a fool? Yet he will be master of all for which I toiled and used my wisdom under the sun. This also is vanity" (Eccles. 2:18–19).

When the writer reflects on the earthly end of animal and human life, he says: "All go to one place. All are from the dust, and to dust all return" (Eccles. 3:20). The allusion to Genesis 3:19 is obvious. In a Genesis 3 world, creation has been "subjected to futility, not willingly, but because of him who subjected it" (Rom. 8:20). Since we are part of creation, we must reckon with the reality of futility in our own lives. The writer of Ecclesiastes speaks as if all of us came from the dust, and thus we share the earthly destiny of humanity's head.

Let's connect the promise of "to dust you shall return" with the earlier warning about the forbidden tree in Genesis 2:17, that "in the day that you eat of it you shall surely die." Having eaten from the tree of the knowledge of good and evil, Adam would be exiled from the garden, and exile from the garden would mean death. The man and the woman would die physically, just not in Eden. The serpent had denied the consequence, but he lied (3:4). God had commissioned the man and woman to exercise dominion and subdue creation, but now they would be overcome by death. They would not subdue the grave. Adam learned that the dust would subdue him. Death would have dominion. In the words of Genesis 3:17–19, God was essentially saying to Adam, "You shall surely die."

While the effects of sin meant death for the couple outside Eden, they would first experience the blessings of work and childbearing (Gen. 3:16–19). These blessings, however, would be tainted with pain. Throughout the genealogy in Genesis 5, the shadow of death looms over the names. Readers will notice the refrain of "and he died" (see 5:5, 8, 11, 14, 17, 20, 27, 31). This is the only genealogy in the Bible with this refrain. The record of death is loud and clear.

The future seed of the woman would be God's answer to a world subjected to futility and death. The disobedience of the first Adam brought death and subjugation, but the obedience of the last Adam would bring life and liberation. The victorious son was Lamech's hope when he named his own son Noah: "Out of the ground that the LORD has cursed, this one shall bring us relief from our work and from the painful toil of our hands" (5:29). Lamech knew the consequences but also the hope that had sounded in the garden.

Crowning the Christ

"The Word became flesh" (John 1:14) in order to deliver sinners from bondage and corruption. Jesus came to surely die. He died so that we will not perish in our sins. We can, instead, embrace the glory and life for which we were made. Growing up in the house of a carpenter, Jesus knew the toil and sweat of work. He was experiencing the Genesis 3 world.

Near the end of his earthly ministry, Jesus was before Pilate, soon to be crucified. After a flogging, Jesus endured an action that the soldiers meant as mockery. "And the soldiers twisted together a crown of thorns and put it on his head and arrayed him in a purple robe" (John 19:2). The soldiers had ill intentions. They were not trying to make a theological point. But in the providence of God, they acted out a truth they failed to recognize.

Not only was Jesus the promised King who had come to lay down his life; he had come to bear the curse and consequence of our sins. He had come to satisfy divine judgment. And there among the soldiers was Jesus, wearing a crown of thorns they had hastily made as they humiliated and demeaned him. Yet there among the soldiers was the seed of the woman who had come to bear the curse upon his head.

Jesus had come to surely die and then to surely rise. He had come to defeat death, to exercise dominion over the dust. He would be the first to enter death and defeat it from the inside, rising again with glory and immortality, an embodied life without end.[1] As believers, we may share the same earthly end as the first Adam, but we will experience vindication like the last Adam. Jesus could say with a straight face to Martha: "I am the resurrection and the life. Whoever believes in me, though he die, yet shall he live, and everyone who lives and believes in me shall never die. Do you believe this?" (John 11:25–26).

The resurrection of Jesus on the third day proved the language of Psalm 16:9–10:

> Therefore my heart is glad, and my whole being rejoices;
> my flesh also dwells secure.
> For you will not abandon my soul to Sheol,
> or let your holy one see corruption.

Jesus is the Son of David, the holy anointed one. Corruption did not claim him, and because of our union with him, it will not claim us either. His resurrection life begins in us spiritually now and then physically at his return.

We, like Adam, have a temporary layover with death. But our bodies will not be forsaken in the dust. The dust will hold our bodies secure until the trumpet sounds.

This Christian Life

A disciple of Jesus lives "under the sun" and thus with the thorns and thistles. In the moments when we're most soberminded about our

---

1 For an exploration of the embodied immortality for which we were made, see Mitchell L. Chase, *Resurrection Hope and the Death of Death*, Short Studies in Biblical Theology (Wheaton, IL: Crossway, 2022).

present and future, we can sense the fleeting and futile nature of life. James 4:14 says we're a mist that appears for a little while and then vanishes. Vanishes where? Genesis 3:19 has an answer: we go to the dust.

Do the consequences of Genesis 3:17–19 devalue life? By no means. Should we turn inward and just live for ourselves since our days are numbered and death is certain? May it never be! This life matters. We matter. The people around us matter. We are image bearers and ambassadors of the living God. In the same book where the author expounds on the reality of our mortality, he ends with this exhortation: "The end of the matter; all has been heard. Fear God and keep his commandments, for this is the whole duty of man. For God will bring every deed into judgment, with every secret thing, whether good or evil" (Eccles. 12:13–14).

We can flourish in a life that is good when it is a life that knows God. We can face the truth of our vulnerable and fleeting days and not collapse in utter despair and fear. To live is Christ, and to die is gain. The wise writer says, "And I commend joy, for man has nothing better under the sun but to eat and drink and be joyful, for this will go with him in his toil through the days of his life that God has given him under the sun" (Eccles. 8:15). There is real joy under the sun—joy in the living God, joy in things small and great. We don't need to fear our earthly pilgrimage to the dust. In Genesis 2:7, God brought life from the dust, and he will do it again when the tombs empty out on the day of resurrection. The last Adam has subdued death, and so will we. The crown of thorns was his so that the crown of life would be ours.

11

The Mother of All Living

TO THIS POINT I HAVE USED the name Eve without any qualification or explanation, as if that was her name from the beginning. But let's read closely. In Genesis 2:22, God makes the woman and brings her to the man. In 2:23, Adam declares,

She shall be called Woman,
   because she was taken out of Man.

In 2:25 the narrator refers to the couple as "the man and his wife." In 3:1 and 3:4 the serpent speaks to "the woman," and in 3:2 "the woman" responds to the serpent. It is "the woman" who sees that the tree is good for food and eats of it (3:6). The man and "his wife" hide themselves (3:8). Adam blames "the woman whom you [God] gave to be with me" (3:12). God questions "the woman," and "the woman" responds (3:13). God speaks about consequences for "the woman" (3:16). Adam has listened to the voice of his "wife" (3:17).

This brief review leads us to a moment in Genesis 3 when Adam gives his wife a name. The one who gives the name, the receiver of the name, the meaning of the name, and the timing of the name are all significant. This woman of God and wife of Adam is called Eve. And the scene pulses with faith and hope. The presence of faith and hope is a welcomed relief to the tension caused by the couple's rebellion, hiding, blame shifting, and consequences.

The Woman

The opening chapter of Genesis declares that God created male and female (1:27). The second chapter of Genesis gives more insight into how this took place. God "formed the man of dust from the ground and breathed into his nostrils the breath of life, and the man became a living creature" (2:7). The Hebrew word translated "man" here also gives us the name Adam. When God created "the man," he created "the Adam." The man was made from the ground, and the Hebrew word for ground is related to the name. God made the *adam* from the *adamah*.

Then in Genesis 2:22, the Lord makes the woman from the man. The word for "woman" is *ishah*, and it sounds like another word for man (*ish*). When the Lord presented her to Adam, the man said:

> This at last is bone of my bones
> > and flesh of my flesh;
> she shall be called Woman,
> > because she was taken out of Man. (2:23)

Adam thus explains the word "Woman." It has to do with her origin. She would be called *ishah* because she came from the *ish*. The word "woman," then, signifies her common humanity with Adam. And just as the man was known as Adam, the woman was probably known as Ishah. It wouldn't have sounded strange for her to call her husband "Adam," and it wouldn't have sounded strange for him to call his wife "Ishah."

God had given the woman to the man in Genesis 2:22 after saying, "It is not good that the man should be alone; I will make him a helper fit for him" (2:18). To be a "helper fit for him" means to be a helper corresponding to him. There was a fittedness or a complementarity to their relationship. They were different from the animals, which did not bear the divine image. Together the *ish* and the *ishah* were to exercise dominion and subdue creation (1:28). They would be fruitful and multiply. They would walk in worship with their Creator.

Though Adam was the head of the human race, the serpent came to the woman with deceptive and tempting words, in order to bring disorder. The woman became a sinner, deserving of judgment. But she was not struck dead. She learned that she would bear children, though through pain (Gen. 3:16). And a future offspring of hers would defeat the serpent (3:15). The woman who sinned became a woman with hope.

Who, What, When, Where, Why

Name changes in Scripture are significant. In *Run with the Horses*, Eugene Peterson reflects on the act of naming:

> Names not only address what we are, the irreplaceably human, they also anticipate what we become. Names call us to become who we will be. A lifetime of growth and development is announced by a name. Names *mean* something. A personal name designates what is irreducibly personal; it also calls us to become what we are not yet.[1]

---

1 Eugene Peterson, *Run with the Horses: The Quest for Life at Its Best* (Downers Grove, IL: InterVarsity Press, 2019), 27.

Let's look outside Genesis 3 for a moment and consider some names. In Genesis 12, we meet Abram and Sarai. But in Genesis 17:5 and 17:15, they are renamed Abraham and Sarah. In Genesis 32, God tells Jacob, "Your name shall no longer be called Jacob, but Israel, for you have striven with God and with men, and have prevailed" (32:28). Abram is renamed, Sarai is renamed, and Jacob is renamed—all by God. What might surprise us in Genesis 3, though, is that God isn't the one who names the woman.

Adam is the one who names the woman. This isn't his first bout with naming either. Genesis 2 says:

> Now out of the ground the LORD God had formed every beast of the field and every bird of the heavens and brought them to the man to see what he would call them. And whatever the man called every living creature, that was its name. The man gave names to all livestock and to the birds of the heavens and to every beast of the field. (2:19–20)

The man saw animals and then named them. Adam probably called the animal a name that made sense in light of what he saw and assessed.

Forward now to Genesis 3. Much has happened and much has changed. Immediately before the naming, God pronounces consequences and curses. Words of judgment hang in the air over the serpent, the woman, and the man. There is no report that God directs the naming. There is no word from the woman about wanting to be addressed differently. And when Adam gives a new name, it's not for himself. *He* is the one naming *her*.

"The man called his wife's name Eve, because she was the mother of all living" (Gen. 3:20). The verse may not be long, but it is packed with significance. Adam did the naming, and his wife received this name. She is called Eve after Genesis 3—in fact, as soon as 4:1! The name Eve means "life" or "living." The meaning of the name is connected to the reason for the name. Adam named her Eve because "she was the mother of all living."

The meaning of the name is important because Adam and Eve didn't have any children yet. But the name signaled his confidence that they would. She had been told about pain in childbearing (Gen. 3:16), and they learned that a future Son would crush the head of the serpent (3:15). These promises could come to pass only if God's image bearers had children. Adam's act of naming was a response to divine revelation.

In Genesis 2:17, the Lord had said, "Of the tree of the knowledge of good and evil you shall not eat, for in the day that you eat of it you shall surely die." Yet Eve ate, and then Adam too. Their eating was a theological statement. Each was saying to God, "I don't believe you." After the encounter with the Lord in Genesis 3, they were given hope and a future, even though the dust would receive them at death. Children would come from them, because God said so. A future deliverer would defeat the serpent, because God said so. By naming his wife Eve, Adam was saying to God, "I believe you."

The Nature of Faith

Does an expression of faith from Adam seem strange at this point? Would you expect that the man through whom sin and death came into the world would be in hell and one day be raised for everlasting judgment? The sentiment is understandable. Even the way Paul uses Adam in Romans 5 is negative. Adam's "transgression" (5:14) and "sin" (5:16) and "trespass" (5:17) are highlighted, as well as the result of "condemnation" (5:18).

While Paul casts the surpassing glory of Christ's work against the disobedience of Adam (Rom. 5:12–21), this is no spiritual evaluation of Adam's entire life. Adam lived 930 years, nearly all of them outside the garden (Gen. 5:5). These years should not be evaluated spiritually using only what he did in Genesis 3:6. In 3:20 he named his wife Eve, and this naming was an acted parable. He was responding to promises God had made, and he responded with faith.

As Peterson put it, "Naming is a way of hoping."[2] Because Adam had hope, he named his wife Eve. And the hope he had was that God would fulfill the promise of offspring and, ultimately, a Son of victory. God, not the serpent, was trustworthy. It is reasonable to say that the woman embraced the name Eve because she too believed the promise of God about her future.

Naming, then, showed hope but also submission. The first couple were submitting to God's wisdom and plan. Like believers after them, they had to walk by faith. They would die before seeing the birth of the promised Son. Though the births of Abel and Seth sustained hope that God would raise up offspring, Adam and Eve could not have known how distant the days of Christ would be. But the action in Genesis 3:20 is a display of faith.

Faith is trusting what God has revealed. Faith isn't a leap in the dark. It's a response to revelation. The writer of Hebrews says, "Now faith is the assurance of things hoped for, the conviction of things not seen" (11:1). Biblical hope is reasonable because God doesn't lie. The assurance of things hoped for is based on divine character and

2   Peterson, *Run with the Horses*, 27.

promise. Believers aren't trying to stir themselves up with pie-in-the-sky confidence. If the things God has promised are yet unseen, we can have conviction and confidence that God's promises will come to pass.

Faith is reasonable because it responds to revelation. A life of faith walks humbly before the living God, who will prove unwaveringly faithful to every promise. To have faith is to say to the Lord, "I believe you." The Christian life is a believing life. And the believers who followed Adam and Eve responded with trust as they lived and died. Since no one receives the glory of embodied immortality apart from his or her own bodily resurrection, believers will always die without receiving everything that was promised (see Heb. 11:39–40).

Abraham walked by faith (Heb. 11:8–12, 17–19). God had told him about many offspring that would come from him. He told the old man, "Look toward heaven, and number the stars, if you are able to number them" (Gen. 15:5). Abraham believed the Lord (15:6). God had made a promise, and Abraham trusted what God said. His name change even reflected the divine promise. The name Abraham means "father of a multitude." Eve would be the mother of all living, and Abraham would be the father of a multitude. Reflected in these names is the promise of offspring, and the hope pulsing through these generations would be a promised Son.

The Mothers Eve, Israel, and Mary

While Eve would be the ancestral mother of her physical descendants, she would bear a spiritual motherhood as well. She was the first woman to hope in God. She was the first woman to believe God's promise and behold his faithfulness. She was the first woman to sin and experience shame. She was the first woman to follow God in a fallen world.

Eve was a queen over creation. This royal status was echoed later in Sarah, whose name means "princess." The promised line would come from Eve, go through the family of Abraham and Sarah, and eventually arrive at a woman named Mary who was betrothed to a man named Joseph. Mary is from the Hebrew name Miriam, which can mean "beloved."

The time span from Eve to Mary is long, and the road getting there is full of twists and turns. Along the way arises the corporate bride of the covenant, Israel, God's beloved but sometimes unfaithful wife. Israel was like a new Eve, heading into sacred space yet yielding to temptation and overcome by deceit. Just as Eve had believing and unbelieving children, the nation of Israel consisted of believing and unbelieving Israelites. Nevertheless, like Mary, Israel was the mother of those who were alive spiritually. Through the saints of old, hope for a Messiah continued.

When Gabriel came to Mary with the news of the long-awaited offspring, she was a virgin. Though not sinless, she had found favor with God and submitted to his will (Luke 1:30). She said, "Behold, I am the servant of the Lord; let it be to me according to your word" (1:38). The angel had delivered promises from God, and Mary believed them. She responded to revelation with trust. She was a servant of the Lord, as Israel had been. Just as Israel would be the nation from which the Messiah would come, Mary would be the Israelite through whom he would be born.

Mary was the new Eve. In her womb would be the hope for all the earth. The merging of figures in Revelation 12 probably speaks to the interplay between the stories of Eve and Israel and Mary. John describes what he saw: "And a great sign appeared in heaven: a woman clothed with the sun, with the moon under her feet, and on her head a crown of twelve stars. She was pregnant and was crying out in birth pains and the agony of giving birth" (Rev. 12:1–2). A dragon waited with ominous and murderous intent, standing before the birthing woman "so that when she bore her child he might devour it" (12:4). Then the woman "gave birth to a male child, one who is to rule all the nations with a rod of iron, but her child was caught up to God and to his throne, and the woman fled into the wilderness, where she has a place prepared by God, in which she is to be nourished for 1,260 days" (12:5–6). The dragon was overcome. "And when the dragon saw that he had been thrown down to the earth, he pursued the woman who had given birth to the male child" (12:13). The raging of the dragon was against the woman and "the rest of her offspring" (12:17).

In Revelation 12, is the woman Eve or Israel or Mary? We can notice that John's descriptions evoke each of them. Through the pains of childbirth, a son is born. The evil one seeks the child's destruction. The son is the promised King, for John says that he will rule the nations (Rev. 12:5; cf. Ps. 2:8–9). Being "caught up" to the divine throne is an image of vindication, authority, and enthronement. Yet the fleeing woman has offspring who are in danger, "those who keep the commandments of God and hold to the testimony of Jesus" (Rev. 12:17). So the woman is Eve, but not only Eve. She is Israel, but not only Israel. She is Mary, but not only Mary. She is even the church of Christ, the multinational people of God, who hope in Christ and resist the devil.

Eve was given her name because she would be the "mother of all living" (Gen. 3:20), and these descendants would ultimately include the stars Abraham saw (15:5) and the woman's offspring whom the dragon would despise. Eve is the mother of all those who are spiritually alive.

Eve's Name in the New Testament

While Eve's person is referred to multiple times in Genesis 2–4, her name appears only twice in the Old Testament. The first reference is Adam's act of naming in 3:20, and the other occasion is 4:1, when Adam and Eve conceive their first child. Outside these two references in Genesis, the only other two references to her by name in the Bible are in the New Testament.

First, Eve is mentioned in 2 Corinthians 11:3. The apostle Paul was defending his ministry against false apostles. They apparently accused Paul of weakness and inferiority, and he refused to allow these impressions to seep unchallenged into the psyche of the Corinthians. Paul was committed to the welfare of the Corinthian church, to their flourishing and purity. He said, "For I feel a divine jealousy for you, since I betrothed you to one husband, to present you as a pure virgin to Christ. But I am afraid that as the serpent deceived Eve by his cunning, your thoughts will be led astray from a sincere and pure devotion to Christ" (11:2–3).

Paul was using Eve's deception in Genesis 3 as a warning for the Corinthian readers. If they were not careful, they would be like Eve, deceived by what appeared to be a trustworthy source at the time. The Corinthians needed to maintain a sincere and focused devotion to the Lord, yet the wiles of the false apostles threatened to derail this devotion. Being led astray begins in the "thoughts" (2 Cor. 11:3), just like it did for Eve when she saw that the fruit was good for food and a delight to her eyes (Gen. 3:6).

Second, Eve is mentioned in 1 Timothy 2:13. Paul was discussing orderliness and propriety in the household of God. He emphasized prayerfulness, modesty, and good works (2:8–10). Then he taught that a woman is not to teach or to exercise authority over a man (2:12). He grounded this instruction in Genesis 2–3: "For Adam was formed first, then Eve; and Adam was not deceived, but the woman was deceived and became a transgressor" (1 Tim. 2:13–14).

When Paul wrote about qualified male leadership in churches (1 Tim. 3:1–7), the headship and leadership of Adam in Genesis 2 shaped his thinking. The order of creation clarified the headship of Adam: "For Adam was formed first, then Eve" (1 Tim. 2:13). Though she wasn't yet named Eve when she was formed (Gen. 2:21–22), Paul referred to her as Eve because of Adam's act of naming in Genesis 3:20.

Eve's name is never mentioned in a genealogy. But twice in Genesis and twice in the letters of Paul, the mother of all living is named.

This Christian Life

The naming of Eve matters because responding in faith to God's revelation matters. Amid a distressful and disastrous situation in Genesis 3, God's image bearers showed signs of faith. The man bestowed, and the woman received, a name. They had heard the promise of Genesis 3:15, and they were the first people to believe it.

We need a heart response of faith to what God has made known. As we read the Scripture, we are confronted with the character and ways of the living God. When we trust what he has said, and when we believe the promises he has made, we are living by faith. We are looking with confidence to the promise maker because his character is faithful and true.

United to Christ, we are the spiritual descendants of Eve our mother. The spiritual seed of the woman includes all those who hold to the testimony of Jesus. Though she became a transgressor and her husband with her, they had a living hope in the living God that Eve would be the mother of all living. In God's plan, the woman named Eve would have an offspring named Jesus. He was her hope, and he is ours.

Genesis 3 is not a flattering picture of humanity's head. Adam was there with his wife when she was deceived, and he ate the forbidden fruit as well (3:6). He tried to cover his shame, he hid from the Lord, and he blamed his wife (3:7–12). Then God pronounced consequences upon the image bearers and creation (3:16–19). With so much going wrong so quickly, the man's act in 3:20 was a welcome ray of faith in the dark. Naming his wife Eve was the best thing Adam did in Genesis 3.

12

Garments from God

SINCE WE CAN'T ADEQUATELY COVER our shame and sin, our only hope is that God can and will. Near the end of Genesis 3, we read what might be the most surprising verse after the sin of God's image bearers. We have heard of the consequences for sin (3:16–19), which make sense because of God's righteousness. We have listened to Adam call his wife a new name, which is a sign of hope in their hearts for a promised deliverer (3:20). Now we will behold an action of God, and what he does is an expression of care, mercy, and provision. But it is also the start of something profound and ongoing. A line can be drawn from this divine act to the cross of the Lord Jesus.

New Coverings

When Adam and Eve first sensed their shame and felt too vulnerable in their nakedness, they sewed fig leaves together and made loincloths to cover themselves (Gen. 3:7). Their instinct to do something about their shame is understandable, but their effort was futile. They could not construct anything outwardly that would remedy their problem inwardly.

Only God could remedy their sin. The promised Son of Genesis 3:15 would not be born for many generations, yet a divine act in the garden foreshadowed what Christ would accomplish. "And the LORD God made for Adam and for his wife garments of skins and clothed them" (3:21). If Adam and Eve needed new garments, we might expect the Lord to have given instructions about making new ones or at least supplementing the fig-leaf loincloths. But the maker of the garments is the Maker of the heavens and the earth.

There are several things we're not told before the event in Genesis 3:21. Did Adam and Eve believe they needed new coverings? Did the Lord tell them ahead of time what he was going to do? Did he explain any significance of the garments? Did he tell them how he was going to acquire the new clothes? All we're told is that the Lord made them garments of skin and clothed them.

Because this divine act occurs near the end of Genesis 3, we can understand the garments to be part of preparation for life outside Eden. Adam and Eve would not call the garden their home for much longer. Eve would experience pains in childbirth outside the garden. Adam would experience the toilsome nature of working the ground outside the garden. But the man and woman were ill-suited for the way of life they were about to enter.

Certain conditions in this life require protective clothing. Our bodies need shielding from the elements. Blazing sun, chilling wind, or pouring rain challenge a poorly dressed person. Though God's image bearers had sinned against him, he cared for their well-being, nevertheless. The new garments showed the graciousness of God. In addition, the garments foreshadowed the important role that animals would play in the life of the people of God.

Animal Skins

Think about the fact that God provided "garments of skins" for Adam and Eve. Where did these skins come from? The most reasonable implication is that these garments were animal skins. And that means these skins came by means of animal death. Adam and Eve were clothed by God through the death of an animal.

Genesis 3:21 implies an animal sacrifice. Prior to this there has been no mention in Genesis of sacrifices. But after Genesis 3 there are sacrifices. This act in 3:21 is more than practically beneficial; it is theologically instructive. Across the Bible's storyline, the people of God relate to God through offerings. The sacrifices don't always signify the same thing. Some offerings are for thanksgiving, others address the reality of guilt, and still others celebrate the communion that God has with his people. Some offerings are from animals, and the template for such a notion begins with this garden act.

Significantly, the act of God's animal offering is connected to Adam's prior act of naming. Genesis 3:20 is followed by "And the LORD God made" in verse 21. Seen side by side, these two verses tell us what Adam did and then what God did. Faith and sacrifice are paired together. Adam and Eve are clothed with new garments, and this symbolizes the new faith and hope they had in God's promise. Genesis 3:15 is a promise they enter by faith in 3:20, and now these garments of skins in 3:21 indicate this spiritual state of affairs.

The new garments are a positive development in the narrative. They are God's affirmation of the faith and hope displayed in Genesis 3:20. We shouldn't necessarily assume that Adam and Eve had these garments until their deaths hundreds of years later, but at this juncture in Genesis, the presence of new garments is a sign of grace, confirmation, and provision. Despite their sin, Adam and Eve would continue to live, and this was due to God's grace. This clothing confirmed the couple's trust in God's promise. The skins showed them divine provision for their human need.

God's act in Genesis 3:21 isn't described in detail. The death of an animal—or even animals—isn't stated; it is reasonably implied. The process of making the garments isn't narrated; the outcome is simply announced. We also don't know Adam and Eve's reaction to God's provision. But the result is stated: the new garments "clothed them."

A Pattern of Sacrifice

Cain and Abel were the first two children of Adam and Eve, and they would've learned about sacrifice from their parents. When we read of the sons bringing offerings to the Lord from the flock and the ground (Gen. 4:3–4), the notion of bringing sacrifices to God is assumed. We're not told that the offerings in Genesis 4 were the first things that Abel and Cain sacrificed. Instead, it is reasonable to assume that the practice of sacrificing was already established.

At some point growing up, Cain and Abel would have learned about bringing offerings to God, about the death of animals for a sacrifice. Adam and Eve would have recounted to them what God had done in the garden years earlier. Through the death of an animal, they were covered. A sacrifice as a substitute—this is the idea God was sowing when he clothed his image bearers with garments of skins.

Cain and Abel are illustrations of the truth that sacrifice must be paired with faith, just as the animal death in Genesis 3:21 is connected to the faith expressed in Genesis 3:20. Abel was a man of faith, but Cain was not. Abel's sacrifice was received, but Cain's was rejected (4:4–5).

Cain is a reminder that the seed of the serpent can offer sacrifices too—except they're offered in vain. God is not pleased with the mere mechanics of religion.

The next sacrifice we see offered was from Noah in Genesis 8. Just as Adam and Eve would have guided their children on the subject of offerings, the subsequent generations of believers would have done the same. In the days of Noah—and after the flood—he "built an altar to the LORD and took some of every clean animal and some of every clean bird and offered burnt offerings on the altar" (8:20). Noah was a new Adam, responsible to teach and model for his children the nature and appropriateness of sacrificial offerings.

After Noah, we next read of sacrifices in the life of Abraham. God guided Abraham to the promised land, and Abraham traveled through it. We're told of altars that he built (Gen. 12:7–8). The most surprising sacrificial scene in Abraham's life comes in Genesis 22. There God tells him, "Take your son, your only son Isaac, whom you love, and go to the land of Moriah, and offer him there as a burnt offering on one of the mountains of which I shall tell you" (22:2). Offerings from God's people had involved animals and altars, but now Abraham was hearing this most unusual command.

As Abraham prepared to climb the mountain with Isaac, the son said to his father, "Behold, the fire and the wood, but where is the lamb for a burnt offering?" (Gen. 22:7). Isaac's observation and question are important because they reveal what the boy had gleaned from his parents. He knew what a burnt offering involved.

Abraham responded, "God will provide for himself the lamb for a burnt offering, my son" (Gen. 22:8). When they reached the place, Abraham bound his son and laid him on top of the wood (22:9). An angel of the Lord intervened at the last moment and said, "Do not lay your hand on the boy or do anything to him, for now I know that you fear God, seeing you have not withheld your son, your only son, from me" (22:12). Abraham saw a ram caught in a thicket. This animal would be the sacrifice instead of his son. Abraham named the place "The LORD will provide," because the ram was provided in place of his beloved son.

Because the Lord has made all his creatures, every sacrificial animal is one the Lord has provided. The scene in Genesis 3:21 is the first installment of such provision, when the Lord made garments of skins for Adam and Eve. Through the death of the animal, the Lord provided. Adam and Eve received the provision of the Lord, setting a trajectory of the people who would follow, like Cain and Abel, Noah, Abraham, and so on. Isaac built altars (26:25), as did Jacob (33:20). The patriarchs offered sacrifices, knowing "the Lord will provide."

Outside the promised land, in a place called Uz, a man named Job offered sacrifices on altars. He was not from Abraham's line, but he shared Abraham's faith. Job had a wife and children, and he acted on behalf of them as the head of the family. He would "rise early in the morning and offer burnt offerings according to the number of them all. For Job said, 'It may be that my children have sinned, and cursed God in their hearts.' Thus Job did continually" (Job 1:5).

Do you see the connection in Job's thinking between the offerings and the problem of sin? Sin needs to be covered. The offerings are an acknowledgment that image bearers have sin and that they need forgiveness. But the offering must be paired with the faith of the offerer. We're told in Job 1:1 that Job "was blameless and upright, one who feared God and turned away from evil." Here was a man who trusted God. Here was a man, aware of his need, who offered sacrifices to God as an expression of faith.

The books of Genesis and Job feature people who built altars and offered sacrifices. The pattern of animal offerings and sin coverings is a pattern rooted in the divine act of Genesis 3:21. People need forgiveness, and the Lord would provide.

Offerings at Divine Dwellings

A transition in the sacrificial pattern occurred in the life of the Israelites. After God delivered them from Egyptian captivity, they traveled to Mount Sinai, and there they constructed a tabernacle—a portable dwelling place where sacrifices would be offered (Ex. 35–40). The notion of altars in the lives of the patriarchs—and in the lives of their contemporaries and predecessors—continued with the tabernacle. A bronze altar would be stationed right inside the eastern entrance to the tabernacle courtyard.

Leviticus 1–7 describes different offerings brought to the tabernacle. The Israelites were a people with sin, and their need was forgiveness. They were made for fellowship with God, yet sin alienates the sinner from the holiness of God. This system of sacrifices at the tabernacle was God's gracious invitation to sinners. They could approach his presence through mediators, the priests of Israel. The priests would enter the tabernacle, which was a tent formed by layers of coverings. The outer layers of the tabernacle covering were made of "tanned rams' skins and a covering of goatskins on top" (Ex. 26:14). As the mediators of Israel entered the tabernacle, they were surrounded by—clothed with—animal skins.

The tabernacle, and later the temple in Jerusalem, contained a sacred room called the Most Holy Place, where God's glory was manifested. The Israelites could not enter the tabernacle unless they were priests, and the only priest who could enter the Most Holy Place was the high priest. These limits of access were a perpetual reminder that the people had sinned and fallen short of the glory of God.

Offerings themselves could not take away sin. There was nothing magical in the blood of an animal that could cleanse a sinner's transgression (see Heb. 10:1–4). The altars and offerings served a temporary role in God's redemptive plan that led to a Roman cross. The death of Jesus was the offering of God's beloved Son upon an altar not of stone or bronze but of wood. The cross-altar was vertical, displaying the sacrifice for all to see.

In Genesis 22, Abraham had nearly sacrificed his beloved son in the land of Moriah. He named the place "The Lord will provide" (22:14). A thousand years later, Solomon built the temple "in Jerusalem on Mount Moriah" (2 Chron. 3:1). Almost a thousand years after that, Jesus died in this region. The cross was where all previous altars and sacrifices were pointing. We picture the hands and feet of Christ fastened to the wood. There was no ram caught in a thicket to be offered at the last moment. Jesus declared his work finished (John 19:30). We can hear the words of Abraham as they echo through millennia to a Friday afternoon in Jerusalem: "The Lord will provide."

A Theology of Clothing

A crucifixion was a scene of shame. The humiliation was public and excruciating. The crucified person was typically stripped naked to increase embarrassment. Roman soldiers had removed Jesus's garments. They "divided his garments among them, casting lots for them, to decide what each should take" (Mark 15:24). While the first Adam was clothed with garments of skin from the Lord, the last Adam suffered unclothed.

Let's think about clothing and shame. When Adam and Eve realized their nakedness, they sewed loincloths to cover themselves (Gen. 3:7), even though earlier they were "both naked and were not ashamed" (2:25). After the fall, shame and nakedness are paired together. The provision of clothing makes the theological point that sin needs to be covered. And the language about uncovering nakedness is typically connected to a wicked act.

For example, in Genesis 9, Noah became drunk and lay naked in his tent (9:21). Ham, Noah's son, "saw the nakedness of his father and told his two brothers outside. Then Shem and Japheth took a garment, laid it on both their shoulders, and walked backward and covered the nakedness of their father. Their faces were turned backward, and they did not see their father's nakedness" (9:22–23). The nakedness needed to be covered by a garment, and Noah's sons Shem and Japheth didn't exploit their father's shame like Ham did.

Clothing was important for Israel's priests. The high priest wore quite lavish garments, complete with beautifully threaded materials and jewels (Ex. 28, 39). God told Israel's mediators, "And you shall not go up by steps to my altar, that your nakedness be not exposed on it" (20:26). Canaanite worship consisted of sexual elements, including nakedness, which is why the Israelites were explicitly told to preserve modesty and propriety. The priests would wear linen undergarments, lest their flowing robes expose their nakedness.

Modesty is fitting for life outside the garden. An immodest situation is provocative in a negative sense. Think of the possessed man in Luke 8. "For a long time he had worn no clothes, and he had not lived in a house but among the tombs" (8:27). Now notice the situation after Jesus delivered the man: "Then people went out to see what had happened, and they came to Jesus and found the man from whom the demons had gone, sitting at the feet of Jesus, clothed and in his right mind, and they were afraid" (8:35). No longer naked, the delivered man was clothed with garments and a sound mind. There is a correspondence between his inner and outer conditions. The clothing was a visible signal that a change had occurred. This new clothing showed there was a new man.

The Christian life is sometimes described as putting on new garments.[1] Paul exhorted the Ephesians to "put on the new self, created after the likeness of God in true righteousness and holiness" (Eph. 4:24). He wrote similar things to the Colossians: "Do not lie to one another, seeing that you have put off the old self with its practices and have put on the new self, which is being renewed in knowledge after the image of its creator" (Col. 3:9–10). The disciple lives in the new garments of new life in Christ.

In this world of spiritual warfare, the believer needs protective garments. We need the whole armor of God, which includes the belt of truth, the breastplate of righteousness, shoes of readiness given by the gospel of peace, the shield of faith, the helmet of salvation, and the sword of the Spirit (Eph. 6:14–17). We need garments that fit the realm in which we live. And we ultimately wrestle not

---

1 Greg Beale notes: "The removing of old clothes and the putting on of new clothes in the OT represents forgiveness of sin (Zech. 3:4–5) or the new eschatological relationship that the people of Yahweh were to have with him after their restoration from Babylon (Isa. 52:1–2; 61:3, 10). Also, new clothes were donned by people when they were installed into positions of rule in the OT (e.g., Joseph in Gen. 41:41–44; Eliakim in Isa. 22:21; Daniel in Dan. 5:29), as well as in the ancient Near East in general. . . . Even in the ancient Near East or in the OT, to receive a robe from a parent or to be disrobed by a parent indicated respectively inheritance and disinheritance." *A New Testament Biblical Theology: The Unfolding of the Old Testament in the New* (Grand Rapids, MI: Baker Academic, 2011), 454n61.

against flesh and blood but against the rulers, authorities, cosmic powers, and forces of evil (6:12).

Paul uses clothing as a metaphor for the human body. This earthly body will die, and that disembodied condition is what Paul calls being "naked" or "unclothed" (2 Cor. 5:3). But believers have a resurrection hope. Though our bodies will return to the dust, we will not be disembodied forever. We were made for embodied immortality in Christ. We long to be "further clothed, so that what is mortal may be swallowed up by life" (5:4). Rising from the dead means getting dressed in everlasting bodily life. In Genesis 3, God provided garments of skins. At the future resurrection, God will provide garments of glory.

In the book of Revelation, the image of washed garments depicts the vindicated and victorious state of God's people. John saw an uncountable multitude from tribes and peoples "standing before the throne and before the Lamb, clothed in white robes" (7:9). The identity of these people is also given: "These are the ones coming out of the great tribulation. They have washed their robes and made them white in the blood of the Lamb" (7:14).

Have you considered how the language about our future life with Christ is never depicted with the nakedness in Eden before the fall? There remains mystery about the appearance of our bodies in the age to come, but language of clothing is applied to our vindicated and resurrected state.

This Christian Life

The events in the garden of Eden aimed forward. When God clothed Adam and Eve with garments of skins, this action communicated both compassion and provision. With nakedness and shame connected, God provided an appropriate covering through animal death.

Fig leaves from the tree would not do. Something better, something long-lasting, was needed. In Matthew Harmon's words, "By providing the sacrifice to cover the sins of Adam and Eve, God establishes a pattern that not only continues throughout the Bible but also anticipates the definitive sacrifice that God will provide—his Son, Jesus Christ."[2]

The many animals across the many years of the sacrificial system could not take away sins. But the truth remained that if sin was ever to be covered, God would have to do it. The work of atonement would have to be a divine work. The trajectory from the animal skins in Genesis 3:21 to the cross in the Gospels is one of pattern and fulfillment. The finished work of Christ has brought an end to burnt offerings.

Now, through faith in Christ Jesus, God has clothed us in the perfect righteousness of Christ. The disciple's life is to keep in step with the truth. We are to become who we already are in Christ. Like getting dressed each day, we have put on the new man—the Lord Jesus. The headship of Adam no longer defines us. The perfect covering of Christ is ours through faith. God sees us as those united to Christ.

Mercy and compassion are what God continually shows sinners. There is a care and tenderness with the language that "God made . . . and clothed them" (Gen. 3:21). He was no debtor to Adam and Eve. But he loved them. He was their Creator and now their coverer. God's heart toward his people is full of steadfast love and mercy. John described the tender action of God wiping away tears as pain and mourning and death pass away in the coming consummation (see Rev. 21:4).

We remember the covering that Christ provided. It is the gospel we preach to our weary souls. While the trees of the garden could not

2 Matthew S. Harmon, *Rebels and Exiles: A Biblical Theology of Sin and Restoration*, Essential Studies in Biblical Theology (Downers Grove, IL: IVP Academic, 2020), 16–17.

shield Adam and Eve from the shame and consequences of their sin, a tree outside Jerusalem gives covering for an uncountable multitude from the nations who seek refuge and pardon. The image of Christ upon the tree is a graphic reminder that the "wages of sin is death" (Rom. 6:23). And the warning of death is rooted in God's own words to Adam early in Genesis: "You shall surely die" (Gen. 2:17).

While God did pronounce consequences for disobedience, his *image bearers* did not die physically there in the garden. The only death in Genesis 3 was of an animal whose skins clothed the couple with garments of grace awaiting glory.

13

East of Eden

AUTHOR J. R. R. TOLKIEN ONCE WROTE in a letter to his son: "Certainly there was an Eden on this very unhappy earth. We all long for it, and we are constantly glimpsing it: our whole nature at its best and least corrupted, its gentlest and most humane, is still soaked with the sense of 'exile.'"[1]

Soaked with the sense of exile. That's a profound evaluation of the fallen human condition. We have desires that aren't satisfied with the things under the sun. We struggle to belong in this world. In our most clearheaded moments, we have a sense that things aren't the way they're supposed to be. The displacement we feel is a sign of the deeper spiritual problem humanity shares. Ever since the events of Genesis 3, all of us have lived east of Eden.

Closing Words

The final three verses of Genesis 3 set up a new beginning, a new trajectory. Verse 22 gives the reason for the action God takes in

---

1   J. R. R. Tolkien, *The Letters of J. R. R. Tolkien*, ed. Humphrey Carpenter (New York: Houghton Mifflin, 2000), 110.

verses 23–24. There was no requirement for God to disclose the reason for what happened next, yet we read an explanation: "Behold, the man has become like one of us in knowing good and evil. Now, lest he reach out his hand and take also of the tree of life and eat, and live forever—" (3:22).

Genesis 3:22 has the last instance of divine speech in the chapter. The writer has given us divine speech in multiple places before this:

- a first question for Adam (3:9)
- two more questions for Adam (3:11)
- a question for Eve (3:13)
- a pronouncement to the serpent (3:14–15)
- a pronouncement to the woman (3:16)
- a pronouncement to the man (3:17–19)

The report in verse 22 is the seventh instance of divine words in Genesis 3. God doesn't ask a question, nor does the writer specify the one (or ones) whom the Lord addresses. Since the divine speeches earlier in this chapter were heard by others, we should probably assume that God gives his reason in the hearing of Adam and Eve too. The words are primarily about Adam, and they first draw attention to the outcome of his sin: "Behold, the man has become like one of us in knowing good and evil."

The notion of "knowing good and evil" makes us think of the forbidden tree and the promise from the serpent. In the midst of the garden, God had planted two trees, and one of them was the tree of the knowledge of good and evil (Gen. 2:9). This was a wisdom tree, for the wise are able not only to discern between good and evil but to commit themselves to what is good and true. All other ground is sinking sand.

The serpent had told the woman, "For God knows that when you eat of it your eyes will be opened, and you will be like God, knowing good and evil" (Gen. 3:5). Does the divine speech in 3:22 confirm that the devil was right? According to 3:7, the "eyes of both were opened." And God says in 3:22 that "the man has become like one of us in knowing good and evil." How should we understand the devil's promise and what actually happened?

Due to the divine action of exile in Genesis 3:23–24, the statement in 3:22 cannot be wholly positive. While Adam knew good and evil, he had an experience with evil that wasn't good. He had transgressed God's commandment. He knew unrighteousness from the inside. God, who is holy and blameless, is perfectly wise. His knowledge of evil is not from experience.

God ensured that Adam would not dwell in Eden as a fallen creature. Adam was to be exiled, "lest he reach out his hand and take also of the tree of life and eat, and live forever" (Gen. 3:22). Now the other tree in the midst of the garden is mentioned. If Adam remained in Eden, his access to the tree of life would continue. Eating the fruit of that tree would apparently sustain him in a mortal and fallen condition. The language "and live forever" clarifies what the fruit from the tree of life would enable.

Even though the woman was the one who took from the tree and ate (Gen. 3:6), God's divine words focused on Adam as humanity's federal head. The last few verses of Genesis 3 tell us that Adam was the only image bearer God addressed and drove out. Now, by implication, if Adam was driven out of Eden, his wife would go with him. If Adam was exiled, humanity was exiled.

The Exile

The biblical author has given us the reason for God's action, and now the action is described: "Therefore the LORD God sent him out from the garden of Eden to work the ground from which he was taken" (Gen. 3:23). Adam's exile meant death. The Lord had warned about what would happen if the image bearers ate from the tree of the knowledge of good and evil: "In the day that you eat of it you shall surely die" (2:17).

To this point in Genesis 3, Adam and Eve were still alive. When they left Eden, they would be bearing a promise of deliverance along with the consequences for sin. Yet the bodies of Adam and Eve were mortal. After being separated from the tree of life, they would surely die. God's warning was no bluff, and Satan was a liar. "You will not surely die," the serpent had told the woman (3:4). But those were deceptive words, directly contradicting the divine words.

The man and woman did die, and their deaths came many years after living with the challenges and vanities of a fallen world. Exile was the path unto death, and the garden was closed to them. God sent out Adam "to work the ground" from which he had come (Gen. 3:23). In Genesis 2:15, Adam had been put in the garden of Eden "to work" its ground. But now Adam's work would be upon the ground that was cursed (3:17).

When the biblical author reminds us that Adam would work "the ground from which he was taken" (Gen. 3:23), this recalls the fact that God "formed the man of dust from the ground" (2:7) and then "put the man" in the garden (2:8). Now in 3:23 the man is being relocated. He will be exiled to the ground from which he was taken. And the dust from which he came would receive him at death (3:19).

While death became a consequence for sin and an enemy to be defeated, it also became a mercy for God's people. Can you imagine living in a toilsome world without end? Can you fathom year after year, century after century, millennium after millennium, with no relief, no liberation, no triumph? Death may bring an end to our mortal bodies, but we have the hope of resurrection. This is why the psalmist says,

Precious in the sight of the LORD
  is the death of his saints. (Ps. 116:15)

This is why the apostle Paul says, "For to me to live is Christ, and to die is gain" (Phil. 1:21).

Because God has the faithfulness and power to keep his promises, death is gain for the people of God. This life is the land of the shadows. We walk—live—through "the valley of the shadow of death" (Ps. 23:4). And though our lives are heading toward the dust, goodness and mercy are not far behind.

To the East

The last verse of Genesis 3 confirms what the previous verse said and gives a little more information: "He drove out the man, and at the east of the garden of Eden he placed the cherubim and a flaming sword that turned every way to guard the way to the tree of life" (3:24). The additional information includes a direction and a guardian.

The angelic guard at "the east of the garden of Eden" implies that the exile was to the east and that reentry would be at that same place. This eastern entrance formed a template for the Israelite tabernacle and temple. When the tabernacle was built, the Israelites entered the courtyard from the east, the priests entered the tabernacle from the east, and the high priest entered the innermost veil from the east. The temple's layout followed this same template.

Eastern entrances on the holy dwelling places among the Israelites, therefore, symbolized a return to Eden. Whenever the priests entered the tabernacle, they were like Adam returning to Eden. Whenever the high priest went behind the veil, he was like Adam returning to the garden paradise. In addition to the tabernacle (and, later, the temple) having an eastern entrance, the Israelites crossed the Jordan River from the east and began the conquest of the land under Joshua's leadership. The land of promise, along with the sacred dwelling places, recalled the days of Eden, when Adam and Eve dwelled in the presence of God with the fullness of blessing and the absence of curse.

When the Israelites rebelled against the commands of God and imitated the worship and ways of the pagan nations, God brought about the judgment of exile he had promised (Deut. 28:32–45; 2 Kings 25:1–21). The Babylonian exile was to the east. The Israelites were like a corporate Adam, evicted from sacred space to face the consequences for rejecting the law of God. And when the exile was over, the Israelites crossed back over the Jordan River from the east. Their return was like reentering Eden.

If readers see the exile of Adam in Genesis 3:24 and wonder whether sinners could ever hope to dwell again with God, the rest of the Bible's storyline is a loud yes. The tabernacle and temple and the promised land all signify hope throughout the epic of God's redemptive plan to pursue and rescue a people for the glory of his name. God is bringing us back to himself.

In Ezekiel 37, the exile of the Israelites to Babylon is a national death, pictured in the prophet's vision as a valley of dry bones. But God makes the bones live (see 37:1–10). The breath of God enters the bones in a work of creation reminiscent of Genesis 2:7. The Lord tells Ezekiel:

> Son of man, these bones are the whole house of Israel. Behold, they say, "Our bones are dried up, and our hope is lost; we are indeed cut off." Therefore prophesy, and say to them, Thus says the Lord GOD: Behold, I will open your graves and raise you from your graves, O my people. And I will bring you into the land of Israel. (37:11–12)

If exile is the way of death, then return from exile is the way of resurrection. What sinners need is pardon from sin and the fruit of the tree of life. In a world marred by corruption and curse, sinners need salvation and bodily life. We dwell east of Eden, and Jesus has come to make the dry bones live. He's come to fill us with new creation breath. As the firstfruits of the resurrection, he is the one who is bringing us out of exile. He's bringing us home because he is the way, the truth, and the life.

Armed Angels

While the biblical storyline signals hope for God's image bearers to dwell with their Maker, the goal is not merely a return to Eden. The Edenic shadows looming over Israel's land and sacrificial system are not meant to hold out a mere return as the desirable end. The garden of Eden was, after all, only the beginning—a trajectory aiming at a global glory project.

The Edenic echoes in the biblical storyline are meant to stir our longing for life with God in unmediated glory and peace, yet this longing will be fulfilled in what God will accomplish as he brings to pass what Eden pointed to all along. Adam's exile from Eden depicted the alienation of image bearers from paradise with God. And the installation of cherubim with a flaming sword was a striking display of seriousness and threat.

Have you thought much about these armed angels? The biblical author says that "at the east of the garden of Eden he [God] placed the cherubim and a flaming sword that turned every way to guard the way to the tree of life" (Gen. 3:24). The word "cherubim" is plural in Hebrew, so we should envision multiple guardians. And their role as guardians is clear by both the weapon and the purpose that the verse reports. There is a "flaming sword" that turns every way "to guard the way to the tree of life."

Adam had been given a responsibility to "guard" (or "keep") the garden ground (Gen. 2:15). But he failed in this task. He didn't guard the sacred space from the unclean lies and presence of the wicked serpent. One way to understand the presence of the cherubim is that they are charged to do what Adam didn't do. As Meredith Kline puts it, "Defiled and driven out, the former priests of Eden were now regarded as themselves potential intruders, against whom the sanctuary must be guarded."[2]

The cherubim were not guarding empty-handed. The flaming sword was a threat of death. No one would enter the garden of Eden and survive. The text doesn't speak of a temporary guard. We should likely imagine that these cherubim were placed there to continually guard the way to the tree of life. An image bearer would have to survive the blade and the flame.

These elements may foreshadow the sacrificial system of Israel. Upon entering the courtyard, the Israelites would bring their sacrifices,

2   Meredith Kline, *Kingdom Prologue: Genesis Foundations for a Covenantal Worldview* (Eugene, OR: Wipf and Stock, 2006), 137.

which would encounter the blade and flame. The animal would be killed and then placed upon the bronze altar to be burned. Significantly, designs of cherubim were woven into some tabernacle materials (see Ex. 36:35). As the Israelites brought their sacrifices to the eastern entrance, the animals were received by blade and flame. This sacrifice represented the worshiper, who needed to be received by God through the sacrificial substitute. Then, representing the worshiper, the priest would enter the tabernacle. And representing all the Israelites on the Day of Atonement, the high priest would go behind the veil and thus through the interwoven cherubim.

We ascend into the presence of God through the designated substitute. The gospel proclaims that Christ is both our offering and our priest. In the garden of Gethsemane, he resolved to drink the cup of judgment in our place. While Genesis 3 tells of unfaithfulness in a garden, the four Gospels tell of faithfulness in a garden. The last Adam came to crush a serpent and redeem a people. He came to reverse the curse.

The Last Word

Have you ever wondered what happened to the garden of Eden? The Bible doesn't tell us. But because cherubim were placed at the east to guard the way to the tree of life (Gen. 3:24), we can reasonably assume that subsequent generations lived with an awareness of this closed paradise. Could they see it? Did anyone ever approach it? Was anyone ever struck down by the flaming sword? No narratives address these things. After the events of Genesis 3, attention turns to life outside Eden.

Since Genesis 6–8 is about the flood that destroys all life on earth that wasn't secured in the ark, we could infer that the flood destroyed Eden as well. Noah emerged from an ark as the new leader of humanity, and God even blessed him and his sons and said, "Be fruitful and multiply and fill the earth" (9:1). This commission echoed Genesis 1:28. But this new Adam—Noah—wouldn't have an Eden. Whatever remained of Eden after Genesis 3 was probably destroyed by the deluge of divine judgment. No one should wonder whether there is an ancient garden, guarded by cherubim, somewhere by the Tigris and Euphrates Rivers.

Genesis 3 ends with a sobering note of exile. But right at the very end—the very last phrase—is "tree of life." That phrase stands as a reminder of what God had placed in the garden and now what sinners were barred from approaching. Adam's exile became our exile. Instead of feasting from the tree of life, God's image bearers would die. But the believers would die holding to the promise of a victorious Son, the seed of the woman.

The Lord Jesus died on the cross and was buried in a garden. Joseph of Arimathea had requested to take Jesus's body from the cross, and, with the help of Nicodemus, he prepared it for burial. "So they took the body of Jesus and bound it in linen cloths with the spices, as is the burial custom of the Jews. Now in the place where he was crucified there was a garden, and in the garden a new tomb in which no one had yet been laid" (John 19:40–41).

When Jesus rose from the dead, he was the last Adam waking up in a garden. Victory was his. The promises had been kept. The tomb was left in the exact condition as when Jesus first entered it—empty. The last word in the garden that day was not death but life. And that last word for Jesus will be the last word for us all. Paul wrote:

> But in fact Christ has been raised from the dead, the firstfruits of those who have fallen asleep. For as by a man came death, by a man

has come also the resurrection of the dead. For as in Adam all die, so also in Christ shall all be made alive. But each in his own order: Christ the firstfruits, then at his coming those who belong to Christ. (1 Cor. 15:20–23)

The voice of the Son of Man will raise the dead. Our mortality is a temporary state. Immortality is coming because Christ is coming, and immortality will be ours because it is his and we are his. So while God's warning that "you shall surely die" (Gen. 2:17) was fulfilled through the onslaught of curse, corruption, and descent to the dust, the last phrase of Genesis 3 tells us what will ultimately be ours from age to age: "the tree of life."

In a chapter narrating disobedience and the rise of the forces of death in God's creation, the last word of the last verse is *life*. While this life would not be ours to demand or earn, it would be ours to receive through faith and promise. The Son of God came to turn the perishing into the living.

This Christian Life

The exile from Eden sets up the story in which we find ourselves. All of us live east of Eden. Our first parents left sacred space with a promise that has been fulfilled. The deliverer has come and defeated death. We are alive in Christ, and our return from exile has begun. And while we are pilgrims in this life, passing through these shadowlands and longing for the age to come, the victory of Christ will be applied on a cosmic scale when death is defeated and all things become new.

Between Eden and the new Jerusalem—this is the space where the disciple of Christ lives. The return of Christ will mean the release of bodies from the bonds of death. "And many of those who sleep in the dust of the earth shall awake, some to everlasting life, and some to shame and everlasting contempt. And those who are wise shall shine like the brightness of the sky above; and those who turn many to righteousness, like the stars forever and ever" (Dan. 12:2–3). We will rise from the dust to glory. We will dwell forever as new creations in the new creation. And we will never be driven out. The resurrection of the dead will mean that, at last, exile has ended.

The apostle John glimpsed the glory that is to come:

> Then the angel showed me the river of the water of life, bright as crystal, flowing from the throne of God and of the Lamb through the middle of the street of the city; also, on either side of the river, the tree of life with its twelve kinds of fruit, yielding its fruit each month. The leaves of the tree were for the healing of the nations. No longer will there be anything accursed, but the throne of God and of the Lamb will be in it, and his servants will worship him. They will see his face, and his name will be on their foreheads. And night will be no more. They will need no light of lamp or sun, for the Lord God will be their light, and they will reign forever and ever. (Rev. 22:1–5)

Do you see how the beginning and ending of the Bible correspond? In the last verse of Genesis 3, we are barred from the tree of life. But in the last chapter of Scripture, the tree of life is ours forever. Because of Genesis 3, the Bible's storyline takes us into a world plagued by the curse of sin and death. But in John's last vision, he sees nothing accursed in the life to come. While our first parents would be alienated from the presence of God in the garden, the vision of John tells of God's people seeing God's face. We have fallen short of the glory of God, but not forever. We will reign in the everlasting light of God.

Conclusion

ONE WAY TO CONCEPTUALIZE the drama of Scripture is to understand the role of Genesis 3 in the storyline. Throughout this book, we have reflected on the content of Genesis 3 in both its immediate context and its canonical context. We have tried to answer several questions along the way: what happened, what does it mean, and why does it matter?

As soon as we read Genesis 3, we cross a threshold with Adam and Eve into a world of thorns and thistles, toil and death. That chapter is not just their story; it's our story too. Paul wrote that "all have sinned and fall short of the glory of God" (Rom. 3:23), and Genesis 3 tells us when this fall took place. Our hope is that the God who justifies us in Christ will glorify us at Christ's return: "And those whom he predestined he also called, and those whom he called he also justified, and those whom he justified he also glorified" (Rom. 8:30).

The reason God plans to glorify his people is that his design in the garden did not change. We were made for a blessed state of existence that was not achieved by Adam and Eve or by those who came after them. John Owen explained:

Man, especially, was utterly lost, and came short of the glory of God, for which he was created. . . . Here, now, doth the depth of the riches of the wisdom and knowledge of God open itself. A design in Christ shines out from his bosom, that was lodged there from eternity, to recover things to such an estate as shall be exceedingly to the advantage of his glory, infinitely above what at first appeared, and for the putting of sinners into inconceivably a better condition than they were in before the entrance of sin.[1]

In the wisdom of God, creation was always heading to consummation. A beginning implied an ending. And God's plan incorporated the fall. His eternal purpose was that through the fallen condition of sinners, the redeeming grace of Christ would display divine mercy and raise his creatures to a blessed estate forever. God will confer glory. John Gill called it "that everlasting glory and happiness which he has prepared for his people, has promised to them, and has called them to by Christ, and will bestow upon them."[2]

God loses nothing by raising us up. His glory does not diminish by our reflecting it in an eternal state. This future is secured in the everlasting love of Christ for his people. He has never not loved us. Christ loved and gave himself for the church that we might be his bride and receive his benevolence. Through the atoning and consummative work of Christ, he will "present the church to himself in splendor" (Eph. 5:27). *Splendor.* God will accomplish such a work in us, and the outcome will be so magnificent, that it warrants words like "splendor."

Our hope is the glory of God (Rom. 5:2). Let the sheer wonder of this notion sink down deep in your heart. You were made for this. You

---

1   John Owen, *The Works of John Owen*, ed. William H. Goold, vol. 2 (Edinburgh: Banner of Truth, 1987), 89.

2   John Gill, *Exposition of the Old and New Testaments*, vol. 8 (1809; repr., Paris, AR: Baptist Standard Bearer, 1989), 449.

were made to behold God. Nothing else will matter more; nothing will be more satisfying. United to Christ in the new covenant, our hearts will exult in and share the glory of the triune God. Only for God is this glory essential. We will forever receive what he so graciously confers.

Glorification is the end of the Christian life, and it serves the same goal as the whole Christian life: the glory of God. By glorifying us, God will glorify himself.

Bibliography

Alexander, T. Desmond. *From Eden to the New Jerusalem: An Introduction to Biblical Theology*. Grand Rapids, MI: Kregel, 2008.

Barcellos, Richard C. *The Covenant of Works: Its Confessional and Scriptural Basis*. Recovering Our Confessional Heritage 3. Palmdale, CA: RBAP, 2016.

Beale, G. K. *A New Testament Biblical Theology: The Unfolding of the Old Testament in the New*. Grand Rapids, MI: Baker Academic, 2011.

Campbell, Constantine R. *Paul and the Hope of Glory: An Exegetical and Theological Study*. Grand Rapids, MI: Zondervan Academic, 2020.

Chase, Mitchell L. *Resurrection Hope and the Death of Death*. Short Studies in Biblical Theology. Wheaton, IL: Crossway, 2022.

Chen, Kevin S. *The Messianic Vision of the Pentateuch*. Downers Grove, IL: IVP Academic, 2019.

Crowe, Brandon D. *The Path of Faith: A Biblical Theology of Covenant and Law*. Essential Studies in Biblical Theology. Downers Grove, IL: IVP Academic, 2021.

Fesko, J. V. *Last Things First: Unlocking Genesis 1–3 with the Christ of Eschatology*. Fearn, Ross-shire, Scotland: Mentor, 2007.

Garrett, Duane A. *A Commentary on Exodus*. Grand Rapids, MI: Kregel Academic, 2013.

Gill, John. *Exposition of the Old and New Testaments*. Vol. 8. 1809. Reprint, Paris, AR: Baptist Standard Bearer, 1989.

Hamilton, James M., Jr. *God's Glory in Salvation through Judgment: A Biblical Theology*. Wheaton, IL: Crossway, 2010.

Hamilton, James M., Jr. "The Skull Crushing Seed of the Woman: Inner-Biblical Interpretation of Genesis 3:15." *Southern Baptist Journal of Theology* 10, no. 2 (2006): 30–54.

Harmon, Matthew S. *Rebels and Exiles: A Biblical Theology of Sin and Restoration*. Essential Studies in Biblical Theology. Downers Grove, IL: IVP Academic, 2020.

Jones, Mark. *Knowing Sin: Seeing a Neglected Doctrine through the Eyes of the Puritans*. Chicago: Moody Publishers, 2022.

Keil, C. F., and F. Delitzsch. *The Pentateuch*. Vol. 1 of *Biblical Commentary on the Old Testament*. Translated by James Martin. Edinburgh: T&T Clark, 1885.

Kline, Meredith. *Images of the Spirit*. Eugene, OR: Wipf and Stock, 1998.

Kline, Meredith. *Kingdom Prologue: Genesis Foundations for a Covenantal Worldview*. Eugene, OR: Wipf and Stock, 2006.

Lewis, C. S. "The Weight of Glory." In *The Weight of Glory and Other Addresses*, 25–46. 1949. Reprint, New York: HarperCollins, 2001.

Morales, L. Michael. *Who Shall Ascend the Mountain of the Lord? A Biblical Theology of the Book of Leviticus*. New Studies in Biblical Theology 37. Downers Grove, IL: InterVarsity Press, 2015.

Morgan, Christopher W., and Robert A. Peterson. *The Glory of God and Paul: Texts, Themes, and Theology*. New Studies in Biblical Theology 58. Downers Grove, IL: IVP Academic, 2022.

Naselli, Andrew. *The Serpent and the Serpent Slayer*. Short Studies in Biblical Theology. Wheaton, IL: Crossway, 2020.

Ortlund, Dane C. "What Does It Mean to Fall Short of the Glory of God? Romans 3:23 in Biblical-Theological Perspective." *Westminster Theological Journal* 80, no. 1 (2018): 121–40.

Owen, John. *The Works of John Owen*. Edited by William H. Goold. Vol. 2. Edinburgh: Banner of Truth, 1987.

Peterson, Eugene. *Run with the Horses: The Quest for Life at Its Best*. Downers Grove, IL: InterVarsity Press, 2019.

Simeon, Charles. "The Seed of the Woman." Discourse 7 in *Horae Homileticae*. Vol. 1, *Genesis to Leviticus*. London: Holdsworth and Ball, 1832.

Tolkien, J. R. R. *The Letters of J. R. R. Tolkien*. Edited by Humphrey Carpenter. New York: Houghton Mifflin, 2000.

Watson, Thomas. *The Ten Commandments*. Carlisle, PA: Banner of Truth, 1965. First published as part of *A Body of Practical Divinity*, 1692.

Young, Edward J. *The Book of Isaiah*. Vol. 2, *Chapters 19–39*. Grand Rapids, MI: Eerdmans, 1969.

General Index

Abel, 23, 117, 127–29, 158, 168
Abraham
  blessing of, 113–14
  died in faith, 16
  as new Adam, 11
  promises to, 10–11
  walked by faith, 159
  willing to sacrifice Isaac, 114, 169
Abrahamic covenant, 16, 77, 80
Abram, renamed, 156
Adam
  blame shifting of, 98–99
  charged to guard or keep the garden,
    10, 186
  disobedience of, 158
  exile from Eden, 51
  failed as prophet, priest, and king,
    71
  failure to serve and guard, 10
  faith of, 157–58
  fear and shame of, 96
  federal headship of, 84–85, 89, 96,
    144, 181
  as first image bearer, 83
  formed from the dust of the ground,
    144
  headship and leadership in, 163
  listened to Eve's words over God's
    words, 142–43

  as priest, 8–9, 51
  rebellion of, 50–51
  subdued by dust, 149
  temptation of, 70–71
  transgression of, 86, 157–58
  as type of Christ, 90
Adam and Eve
  ate fruit from forbidden tree, 24
  became fools, 23
  covenant relationship with God, 81
  exiled from Eden, 10, 27, 181
  hid themselves from presence of
    God, 95–96
  needed new garments, 166
  walked with God, 37
adversary, 57–58
Alexander, T. Desmond, 4n2, 14n5,
    29–30, 48n1
all things become new, 16–17
ancient Near Eastern covenants, 81
angels, 48, 185–86
animal sacrifice, 167
animal skins, 167–68
armor of God, 174

Balaam, 57, 115
Bancroft, Charitie Lees, 62n6
Barcellos, Richard, 89
Beale, Greg, 51n2, 174n1

Scripture Index